The Military History of World War II: Volume 17

COMBAT LEADERS OF WORLD WAR II

by Trevor Nevitt Dupuy

COL., U.S. ARMY, RET.

FRANKLIN WATTS | NEW YORK | LONDON

SBN-531-01249-2

Library of Congress Catalog Card Number: 62-7382
Copyright © 1965 by Franklin Watts, Inc.
Printed in the United States of America

6   7

To my Mother and Father,
This Year of their Golden Wedding Anniversary

Contents

INTRODUCTION	1
AMERICAN ARMY COMMANDERS IN EUROPE, AFRICA, AND ITALY	1
AMERICAN ARMY COMMANDERS IN ASIA AND THE PACIFIC	16
AMERICAN NAVAL AND MARINE COMMANDERS	27
Sailors of the Pacific 27	
Sailors of the Atlantic and Mediterranean	37
The Marines 37	
AMERICAN AIR FORCE COMMANDERS	40
BRITISH ARMY COMMANDERS IN THE FIELD	49
ROYAL NAVY COMMANDERS AT SEA	62
ROYAL AIR FORCE COMBAT COMMANDERS	73
LEADERS AMONG THE OTHER ALLIES	82
Russia 82	
France 86	
China 91	
Smaller Allied Nations 94	
COMMANDERS IN THE AXIS FORCES	96
Germany 96	
Japan 112	
Italy 119	
INDEX	121

Introduction

In the sixteen previous volumes in this series, I have endeavored to present a clear picture of all of the significant events of World War II. In those volumes I have not avoided expressing opinions where I felt these would help the reader to see the events in perspective. But such opinions were secondary to the facts.

The primary purpose of this volume, however, is to concentrate on opinion, without ignoring the facts. Presented here are the judgments of a military historian who personally took part in the war, who has painstakingly reviewed hundreds of references in the preparation of this series, and who has spent the major portion of his life as a military professional.

I have endeavored to be objective and fair; I have sought opinion and advice from fellow military men and historians. But, the selection of those whose names appear in the chapters of this book — as well as the opinions, comments, and evaluations expressed — has been my personal and sole responsibility.

American Army Commanders in Europe, Africa, and Italy

Shortly after America's entry into World War II, newly promoted Brigadier General **Dwight D. Eisenhower** joined the War Plans Division of the Army General Staff in Washington. Early in 1942 Army Chief of Staff General Marshall selected Eisenhower to be the chief of the influential Operations Division, the nerve center through which Marshall planned and controlled all overseas combat operations of the Army. Then in quick succession Eisen-

1

General of the Army Dwight D. Eisenhower (center) with Field Marshal Sir Alan Brooke (left) and Prime Minister Winston Churchill. U.S. Army Photograph

hower was selected to be commander of U.S. forces in England, and commander of the combined American-British army which invaded North Africa. This was "Operation Torch," culminating in the liberation of Tunisia in May, 1943.

Continuing as the Allied commander in the Mediterranean, Eisenhower — now a full, four-star general — controlled the armies which conquered Sicily, and which invaded Italy. At the Cairo Conference (November, 1943) Eisenhower was selected by Roosevelt, Churchill, and the Combined Chiefs of Staff to be the Supreme Allied Commander for the invasion of Europe, which began on June 6, 1944. During the following eleven months his armies liberated France, Belgium, the Netherlands, and Luxembourg, and had overrun all of western and southern Germany at the time of the German unconditional surrender on May 7, 1945. In December, 1944, Eisenhower had been promoted to General of the Army, America's highest military rank.

Eisenhower's detractors claim that he had no real combat command experience and was merely a genial "chairman of the board"; a political general who could get along well with the British and who leaned over backward to avoid interallied and interservice controversies; a man who preferred to settle disputes and to solve problems by compromise rather than by decision; a soldier who failed to understand the basic strategical issues involved in the defeat of Germany, as shown particularly by his failure to seize a clear opportunity to capture Berlin before the Russians. His admirers agree that he understood political affairs, but point out that he was an unparalleled military diplomat who welded a superbly efficient American-British staff, who handled proud and touchy subordinates with finesse, and whose strategic vision and skill were primary factors in the tremendous Allied victories over the Germans in Western Europe.

Both of these points of view are partly right. It took real professional military ability as well as luck and charm to rise as rapidly in the American Army as Eisenhower did in the early months of the war. The results which his armies and air forces achieved are in large part a tribute to his unquestioned organizational, as well as his diplomatic, capabilities. He selected good subordinates, gave them great freedom of action, but retained firm control over them. He did not shrink from making difficult decisions, one of which was one of the toughest in the history of war: the unleashing of his forces for the invasion in the face of the threat of a potentially disastrous storm. Without a doubt, he was one of the most successful military commanders ever produced by the United States.

There is, however, some basis for the criticism that Eisenhower could not make up his mind. Undoubtedly he was keenly aware that he had had no command experience of a unit larger than a company, before he was commanding an army group in battle. Save possibly for his key decision to go ahead with the invasion in the face of the storm threat, he was better at taking advantage of opportunities presented to him than he was in shaping events to make opportunities for himself. He has been criticized by his subordinates Montgomery, Bradley, and Patton, not only for having failed to make a strategic decision for a truly decisive main effort in Western Europe but also for hesitancy in carrying out the more cautious decisions which he did make.

The most controversial of Eisenhower's command decisions was that of stopping his onrushing armies at the Elbe River when they could almost certainly have entered Berlin before the Russians. Instead, he turned the advance into southern Germany for the purpose of preventing the Nazis from establishing a so-called "Alpine Redoubt." Critics say that it should have been obvious that the defeated Germans could not have held the mountains of southern Germany, and that failure to take Berlin set the stage for a major cold-war battleground.

Here the critics are on less solid ground. Eisenhower was acting in accordance with political decisions reached at Yalta, and with political and military guidance he had received from the United States. A Montgomery would have taken Berlin anyway — not because he was a greater general, but because both he and the British government recognized the tremendous political importance of Berlin. A Patton would probably also have taken Berlin, even despite guidance to the contrary, simply because of his military instincts. A MacArthur would have taken Berlin, even under the permissive guidance given Eisenhower, because of his unerring ability to understand complex and interrelated political and military strategic issues. Eisenhower, a responsible and, in many ways, gifted soldier, lacking inspiration from his government, was not himself inspired to a stroke of genius.

Omar N. Bradley was known as the "GI's General" of World War II. This was not because Bradley was a "pal" to the troops — far from it. This quiet, dignified, and austere man would never have thought of trying to make his soldiers like him. But the men loved him for two reasons: first, his simple, natural, courteous, and unaffected manner, which was unchanged by crisis and unvarying whether he was talking to a private or a field marshal; second, a tough, quick, and competent military leadership that won battles with the least possible loss to his men.

Bradley's rise to top-level leadership in the war was typically unspectacular, but quick and sure. After proving his organizational and administrative skill in commanding two newly mobilized

divisions in the United States, he was rushed to Tunisia to take command of the American II Corps, just after it had been badly mauled by Rommel at Kasserine Pass. When the final Allied assault in Tunisia came in May, Bradley's corps was not supposed to have an important mission, but his revitalized Americans stormed into Bizerte ahead of the amazed British.

A few months later, Bradley's II Corps performed with equal credit to him and to his men as part of Patton's Seventh Army in the invasion of Sicily. As a result, Bradley was selected to go to England to take command of the American First Army, which was then preparing to be the American spearhead for the Normandy invasion.

Bradley's skill in the landing, and in the hedgerow fighting that followed, caused Eisenhower to appoint him to command the American 12th Army Group just before the breakout from Normandy. From that time until the end of the war, Bradley's army group made up the central portion of Eisenhower's vast command. When the war ended, with his armies either on the Elbe or sweep-into Czechoslovakia and Austria, Bradley commanded the First, Third, Ninth, and Fifteenth Armies, the largest ground force ever assembled under American leadership.

Bradley was not a colorful man like Montgomery and Patton, who got much more personal publicity; the "GI's General" was a soldier's soldier; a brave, skillful commander, always considerate of the lives of his men, and always reliable, no matter how tough the situation.

Jacob L. Devers was perhaps the forgotten American general of World War II. One of three Americans to command army groups in combat in Europe, he never had an opportunity to take a leading role in any of the more notable events of the war, but from the outset he was one of the principal supporting players.

As a brilliantly successful division commander in the buildup of the American Army in 1940, Devers was placed in command of that Army's new and growing Armored Force just before the outbreak of the war. His outstanding success in the development of American armored forces and armored doctrine led to his appointment as Commanding General of the European Theater of Operations, succeeding Eisenhower. Later, in 1944, he became deputy Supreme Allied Commander in the Mediterranean Theater, under

General Jacob L. Devers.
U.S. Army Photograph

Field Marshal Alexander. Then, in September, 1944, he was placed in command of the newly organized 6th Army Group, consisting of the American Seventh and French First Armies, on the right flank of General Eisenhower's Allied Force Europe. He retained this command until the end of the war.

Devers' army group was responsible for clearing the Germans from Alsace and from the nearby Rhineland provinces of Germany; following this, his armies overran southwest Germany. Devers displayed in these campaigns the same high order of professional ability that had marked his entire military career. His greatest problems — and his greatest successes — were in dealing with touchy General de Lattre de Tassigny, commanding the French First Army, and with even more touchy General de Gaulle, who tried unceasingly (but unsuccessfully) to bypass Devers in the chain of military command over de Lattre.

8

George S. Patton, Jr., was America's most colorful general of World War II, and one of the most controversial. He was one of the few Americans to have combat experience with tanks in World War I; in the years between the wars he became one of the U.S. Army's leading exponents of armored warfare. His first important mission in World War II was as commander of the Western Task Force in "Operation Torch," in which he quickly and efficiently overwhelmed the Vichy-French defenders of Morocco. He next commanded the American Seventh Army in the invasion of Sicily,

General George S. Patton, Jr.
U.S. Army Photograph

9

an operation in which his theatrical flamboyance and his hard-driving military skill received equal press attention. Particularly spectacular was his armored drive which captured Palermo. An emotion-charged incident in which Patton slapped a hospitalized soldier whom he suspected of trying to avoid combat received even greater attention, however. Because of the fuss caused by this incident, Eisenhower relieved him of his command, and Patton went into temporary eclipse.

Patton's sun rose again, however, with greater brilliance, when his newly established American Third Army broke through the German lines around the Normandy beachhead in late July, 1944. This was the beginning of one of the most thrilling pursuits in the history of war, and "Old Blood and Guts" drove himself and his men in a ruthless chase after the defeated Germans across north-central France. The pursuit ended in mid-September, when Patton's army, approaching the German frontier near Metz, ran out of gasoline.

Forced by lack of supplies to remain relatively quiet until mid-December, Patton had just begun a new offensive when the German breakthrough in the Ardennes caused Bradley to order the Third Army to strike north against the southern side of the "Bulge." In an amazing display of operational and logistical skill, Patton changed the direction of his attack by 90 degrees in less than twenty-four hours, and in a blinding blizzard drove north to relieve Bastogne on Christmas Day.

His next exploit was another example of operational and administrative skill in an armored and infantry drive through the Rhineland in close coordination with the Seventh Army. Following this, his army was supposed to halt, while the main Allied effort was to be made by Montgomery's British-American 21st Army Group.

But, without the knowledge or permission of his superiors, Patton secretly crossed the Rhine a hundred miles to the south, one day before Montgomery's long-planned and carefully rehearsed crossing. Patton then began another vigorous armored drive to the east and northeast, first linking up with Simpson's Ninth Army to surround more than 500,000 Germans in the Ruhr, and then driving eastward. His army's spearheads halted in Czechoslovakia and Austria shortly before the German surrender.

Patton was one of the great field commanders of American history, taking a place alongside such flamboyant and competent soldiers as "Stonewall" Jackson, Nathan B. Forrest, and Philip Sheridan.

Shortly after World War II Winston Churchill stated that it was "a wonder of military history" how America's small prewar army was expanded in a short time to a "mighty force of millions of soldiers . . . victorious in every theater. . . ." He added that it was "a mystery as yet unexplained" that this expanded army could find leaders "capable of handling enormous masses and moving them faster and farther than masses have ever been moved in war before. . . ."

Among those leaders whom Churchill had specifically in mind were men like Generals **Courtney H. Hodges, William H. Simpson,** and **Alexander M. Patch, Jr.** These competent and successful soldiers commanded armies in Western Europe under Montgomery, Bradley, and Devers. Hodges' First Army was known as "the workhorse of the AEF"; he and his staff had a reputation in the European Command of being the most professional group of military men in Europe. The capability of Simpson and of his army is made obvious by the fact that Montgomery chose them to spearhead his

11

General Alexander M. Patch, Jr.
U.S. Army Photograph

last great drive into central Germany. Patch, who first made a name for himself as the conqueror of Guadalcanal, added to his reputation by his brilliant record in command of the U.S. Seventh Army in the amphibious landing in southern France (August, 1944), the subsequent pursuit of the Germans up the Rhone Valley, and in operations in Alsace, the Rhineland, and southern Germany in the final months of the war.

General Mark W. Clark with Prime Minister Churchill reviewing troops of the Fifth Army on the Italian front.
U.S. Army Photograph

Mark W. Clark first attracted fame in October, 1942, when he made a successful and dramatic submarine trip to Algeria for secret conferences with French officers before the Allied landings in November. His command reputation, however, was made in Italy. He led the American Fifth Army in the invasion of Italy at Salerno, in September, 1943, and remained in command of that army in the tough, dreary campaigns that followed. He is the only American

13

ever to have captured Rome. After leading the Fifth Army through Florence, he was promoted to command the Allied 15th Army Group, and thus was responsible for the final Allied land victory in Italy in the spring of 1945.

Clark had a reputation for being a "grandstand" player, and unquestionably personal publicity and concern for his own reputation influenced some of his decisions. There have been serious criticisms of his part as Army commander in the planning and conduct of the Anzio landing and in the simultaneous operations along the Rapido. This latter criticism of Clark's leadership, mostly by the disgruntled men of the 36th Division (Texas National Guard), seems totally unwarranted. He properly insisted upon the division's maintaining pressure at the Rapido, even after they had been repulsed by the Germans, for the highly proper purpose of preventing the Germans from concentrating decisive strength at Anzio.

On balance, Clark ranks high among the American leaders who so amazed Churchill.

Lucian K. Truscott was a no-nonsense "soldier's soldier." He commanded a brigade in North Africa, and then trained and led the 3rd Infantry Division in Sicily and in the early campaigns in Italy, making a reputation as the best division commander in the theater. When things went wrong at Anzio, Clark put him in as VI Corps commander. Truscott's firm leadership and defensive skill halted, then repelled, the nearly successful German efforts to wipe out the beachhead. After leading the VI Corps in its successful breakout from the Anzio beachhead in the Rome campaign (June, 1944), Truscott and his corps were chosen to be the spearhead of General Patch's Seventh Army in the amphibious assault on southern France (August, 1944). His brilliant, unorthodox, and

Lieutenant General Lucian K. Truscott.
U.S. Army Photograph

improvised pursuit after that landing smashed the German Nineteenth Army defending southern France. He went back to Italy in December to take command of the Fifth Army after Clark moved up to the 15th Army Group. Truscott's army spearheaded the final successful conquest of Italy.

General Truscott has the distinction of having written the best memoirs of any American general of World War II (*Command Missions*, New York, 1954). His trim, soldierly, direct prose, and his objective analyses of the operations in which he took part, are fully consistent with the superb leadership he displayed in those operations.

American Army Commanders in Asia and the Pacific

THE MOST controversial American military figure of World War II was **Douglas MacArthur.** His admirers are extravagant in their praise, and most of them seem to think that he could do no wrong. His critics admit that he had some ability, then try to find all possible reasons to discredit him as a man, as an American, and as a soldier.

The son of a famous American soldier, MacArthur rose to the rank of brigadier general and division commander in World War I and remained active as a general officer for thirty-three years. His fabulous career was filled with more adventure, romance, and honors than would be believable in the wildest romantic fiction. Profusely decorated for heroism and skillful leadership in World War I, MacArthur's subsequent distinguished career included five unprecedented years as Chief of Staff of the Army, followed by six years as commander of the armed forces of the Philippine Commonwealth. In 1941, because of the threat of war with Japan, he was recalled to active duty in command of all United States and Philippine Army forces in the Far East.

Although not outnumbered, his inexperienced and ill-equipped troops were completely outmatched by the veteran Japanese forces invading the Philippines in December, 1941. MacArthur's concentration of his scattered units, and his withdrawal to planned defensive positions on the Bataan Peninsula, were brilliant military feats, as was the subsequent defense of Bataan by his poorly nourished troops. It is noteworthy that there were four important amphibious landings which failed in World War II; all of these were Japanese assaults against MacArthur's troops, and three of them occurred during the defense of Bataan.

16

General of the Army Douglas MacArthur. U.S. Signal Corps Photograph

MacArthur, after ignoring one order to leave the Philippines, finally obeyed the personal command of President Roosevelt to go to Australia to become commander of all Allied forces in the Southwest Pacific Area. In the following two and a half years he led a spectacular Allied drive from the shores of Australia to the heart of Japan. Some of the operations — such as Lae, Hollandia, and the Admiralties — bore a stamp of genius unexcelled elsewhere on either side in World War II. In the process MacArthur established himself as one of the three or four greatest generals in American history; a leader worthy of comparison with the great military captains of all time.

17

In the process MacArthur also gained a reputation as a self-centered publicity-seeker. Despite sound common sense in most matters, there can be no doubt that MacArthur craved glory. This weakness was magnified by another. Although he was unerring in the selection of his principal subordinate combat commanders — men like Krueger, Eichelberger and Kinkaid — he often chose petty flatterers for his personal staff. These men, anxious to please the great man, tried to build up his publicity, often merely to gain some reflected glory for themselves.

Because of MacArthur's vanity, and because of his later dispute with President Truman (in which MacArthur was wrong as an American general, though perhaps right as an American citizen), the general has been pictured as a potential dictator; a "man on horseback"; a threat to American democracy. This is wrong. Mac-Arthur's devotion to the American Republic and to its democratic processes is unquestionable. He was an autocrat; he was never a potential dictator.

Despite the continuing efforts of lesser men to try to diminish the scope of his tremendous victories and his part in them, despite other efforts to attempt to cast on him blame for various setbacks and blunders, the record is clear. No soldier has better or more faithfully served his nation in peace or war. MacArthur was the greatest general of World War II.

Jonathan M. Wainwright, IV, was the senior American military man under MacArthur when the Japanese invaded the Philippines in December, 1941. "Skinny" Wainwright commanded Mac-Arthur's I Corps of mixed American and Philippine units. He and his men performed magnificently in so delaying the Japanese advance as to permit MacArthur to carry out his plan of concentrat-

18

General Jonathan M. Wainwright, IV.
U.S. Signal Corps Photograph

ing his forces on the Bataan Peninsula. Wainwright continued to perform with comparable efficiency as MacArthur's principal subordinate in the defense of Bataan, and later as the commander of all forces in the Philippines, after MacArthur was ordered to Australia.

The overwhelming superiority of the Japanese, and the weakness of his own starving troops, forced Wainwright to surrender Bataan and Corregidor to the Japanese. He remained a prisoner of war until August, 1945. He was rescued in time to join MacArthur at the Japanese surrender on the battleship USS *Missouri*, September 2, 1945.

Wainwright was a competent, dependable, honorable American soldier, who suffered disaster with dignity, but not with equanimity.

General Joseph W. Stillwell.
U.S. Army Photograph

"We got a hell of a beating . . ." said General **Joseph W. Stilwell**, after hiking over the jungled mountains between Burma and India in the monsoon rains of 1942. "We got run out of Burma and it is as humiliating as hell. I think we ought to find out what caused it, go back and retake it."

And that is what Stilwell did. He was not present at the final victory in North Burma in the spring of 1945, since he had been ordered back to the United States in October, 1944, after a political squabble with Generalissimo Chiang Kai-shek of China. But the final successful plan was Stilwell's, and the victory was his without question — as Chiang acknowledged when he celebrated the opening of the Stilwell Road from India, through North Burma, into China.

Stilwell was a soldier, not a diplomat. It was a political error to put him in a position as commander of the American China-Burma-India Theater where he had to maintain good relations with allies — the Chinese and the British. He failed seriously in this diplomatic mission.

But, as a fighting man, the commander of a mixed bag of Chinese, American, and British troops attempting to reconquer Burma, Stilwell was a complete success. He had detractors and enemies — many of them. Not for nothing was his nickname "Vinegar Joe." As he personally inspired his Chinese troops to fight against the Japanese more successfully than they or anyone (except Stilwell) thought was possible, officers in soft rear-area billets spoke sneeringly of him as "the best three-star battalion commander in the American Army." He was accused of making plans without any understanding of logistical problems and then asking his troops to make unnecessary sacrifices to make up for his planning weaknesses.

But the soldiers of all three countries who fought under his command in Burma knew very well that he could not only command a battalion; he proved himself an inspired and inspiring leader of a tri-national army as well. As to his logistical shortcomings, no combat units under his command were ever seriously handicapped by shortages of supplies. Though some of his troops suffered severe losses in the taking of Myitkyina, no one (again except for Stilwell) had thought that he had a chance of taking the city in 1944 under any circumstances.

General Walter Krueger.
U.S. Army Photograph

One of the many enemies Stilwell made in Asia was hard-fighting Air Corps General Claire L. Chennault. Chennault and his flyers accused Stilwell of not understanding the capabilities of air power. Chennault was probably the greatest aerial tactician of World War II; but Stilwell, by recognizing its limitations, proved himself a more competent judge of air power than the flyer was.

When MacArthur asked to have Lieutenant General **Walter Krueger** sent to his Southwest Pacific Command early in 1943, the request was denied because Krueger was over sixty years old, and thus considered to be unfit for the rigors of field operations. Mac-Arthur insisted, and Krueger joined him, to take command of the Sixth Army. Prussian-born Krueger had a reputation as the American Army's most able peacetime tactician, as well as its strictest and most feared disciplinarian; his record with the Sixth Army showed that these qualities paid dividends in combat.

For two years Krueger's army was MacArthur's principal striking force — in New Guinea, New Britain, Leyte, and Luzon. Its invariable success, against the finest troops of the Japanese army, with the lowest major-war combat-loss-ratio in history, is testimony not only of MacArthur's strategic wizardry, but also of Krueger's superb tactical and administrative skill. The man who was too old to go to war proved himself to be unselfish, modest, brilliant, and completely professional as one of the finest field army commanders in American history.

Lieutenant General **Robert L. Eichelberger** proved himself as a combat leader when MacArthur sent him to take over the stalled American-Australian force that had been thrown back on its heels by the grim Japanese defense of Gona-Buna, late in 1942. (The Australians were tough veterans, but the Americans were inexperienced, and close to demoralization in the face of Japanese counterattacks.) Eichelberger quickly reestablished morale, trained his troops to fight effectively together by carefully planned limited attacks, then resumed the offensive to win one of the first important Allied victories of the Pacific War.

When the Eighth Army was established in September, 1944, MacArthur placed Eichelberger in command. The Eighth Army was continuously in action for the next year: in the southern Philippines, in Borneo (where mostly Australian troops were engaged),

General Robert L. Eichelberger.
U.S. Army Photograph

and in the conquest of Luzon. No greater praise can be given Eichelberger than to say that he was a worthy partner to Krueger.

Simon Bolivar Buckner, Jr., was the son of the unfortunate Southern commander to whom U. S. Grant sent his famous message: "No terms but unconditional surrender!" The younger Buckner commanded in only one major operation: Okinawa. Although the ultimate American victory was perhaps a foregone conclusion, this audacious venture, thousands of miles from the nearest American base, and close to the shores of Japan, was no certain American success when it began, despite overall American air and naval superiority. Finding himself opposed by the best-prepared Japanese army encountered during the entire war, Buckner decided to avoid risky tactics.

When held up by the Japanese in May, 1945, he was criticized for his refusal to undertake an amphibious turning movement behind the Japanese lines, against southern Okinawa. Perhaps remembering what had happened at Anzio, he decided to keep his forces concentrated and to smash through the enemy defense in a manner reminiscent of the tactics of his father's conqueror. He was as successful as Grant had been tactically, and for much the same reason; yet this writer believes that if a Grant had had a similar opportunity, he would have made the turning movement, and would probably have won the battle a month earlier.

On June 18, 1945, Lieutenant General Buckner visited a forward observation post, near the southern tip of Okinawa, just as his Tenth Army was making its final assault on the last Japanese stronghold of the island after two and a half months of slow advance against bitter enemy resistance. A Japanese shell struck the observation post, killing the commanding general instantly.

Upon the relief from command of General Stilwell in October, 1944, relatively young Major General **Albert C. Wedemeyer** was promoted to lieutenant general and sent to China to take over Stilwell's former post as chief of staff to Generalissimo Chiang Kai-shek, and as commander of American forces in China. Wedemeyer had had no previous combat experience, having risen rapidly from the rank of major at the outset of the war because of his flair as a brilliant strategic planner.

At the time Wedemeyer took over, China was reeling under the impact of a sustained Japanese land offensive which — as Stilwell had predicted — Chennault's strengthened air force was unable to stop since insufficient American support had been given to the Chinese armies in China. Wedemeyer, a consummate diplomat, quickly gained the confidence of Chiang, Chennault, and of the senior Chinese generals. Obtaining additional supplies for the shaken Chinese armies, Wedemeyer bolstered them by shifting two of Stilwell's best Chinese divisions from Burma. Then he ordered a counterattack. With Chennault's support, the Japanese were first

General Albert C. Wedemeyer.
U.S. Army Photograph

stopped, then pushed back. Wedemeyer then started an offensive which continued until the Japanese surrender, some six months later.

Best known — and rightly so — for his skill as a planner and as a staff officer, Wedemeyer demonstrated in China in 1944–45 that he was a talented commander. It is particularly to his credit that he was able to achieve the results that he did, so shortly after the quarrel between Chiang and Stilwell, and under circumstances in which he could exercise command only by advising and suggesting operations to the Generalissimo.

American Naval and Marine Commanders

SAILORS OF THE PACIFIC

DOMINATING THE naval picture in the Pacific from the time of the initial disaster at Pearl Harbor until the final Japanese surrender in Tokyo was Admiral **Chester W. Nimitz.** Taking over command of the Pacific Fleet from unfortunate Admiral H. E. Kimmel on December 31, 1941, Nimitz directed the naval and amphibious operations of the Pacific Ocean Areas from his Pearl Harbor headquarters.

Nimitz did not have a chance to prove himself as a naval tactician; like Eisenhower, he reached the pinnacle of supreme command without having had the opportunity to command tactical forces in combat. But as the architect of the most decisive battle of the Pacific War — Midway — he earned for himself a firm position in the Pantheon of the great admirals of history. Thanks to "Magic," the United States' code-breaking ability to decipher Japanese secret radio messages, Nimitz learned in advance of the

27

Fleet Admiral Chester W. Nimitz.
U.S. Navy Department

Japanese plans for the thrusts through the Coral Sea and against Midway. Decisively and daringly, Nimitz shuttled his vastly outnumbered forces across the reaches of the Pacific, first stopping the Japanese southward movement at the Battle of the Coral Sea, then reassembling his ships in time to strike a totally unexpected and paralyzing counterblow at Midway. There he ended forever Japanese control over the Central Pacific, and began the change in the tide of war which did not end until he participated in the final surrender ceremony in Tokyo Bay.

Nimitz was one of the great admirals of history, but in the tradition of Themistocles — the first outstanding naval commander — rather than of Nelson or John Paul Jones. A calm, soft-spoken man, he had the vision, will, determination, and professional skill to shape victory from afar, making the best possible use of subordinates in the process.

The first of Nimitz' two principal subordinates was **Raymond A. Spruance,** whose tactical skill and brilliant, quiet leadership were fully comparable to Nimitz' strategic vision. An outstanding naval commander in his own right — perhaps one of the very greatest produced by the United States — the fortunes of war placed

Admiral Raymond A. Spruance.
U.S. Navy Photograph

Spruance in positions where he had numerous opportunities to prove his seamanship and fighting abilities as an independent commander; but he never had a chance to exercise supreme strategic command himself.

Spruance first showed his ability in the Battle of Midway, when Admiral W. F. Halsey was ill, and Admiral Frank J. Fletcher's *Yorktown* was mortally damaged by Japanese planes. This left Spruance — still a relatively junior admiral — to continue the battle with the two remaining American carriers. Thanks largely to his selection of the right time to launch his attack, in a few hours Spruance's planes destroyed four Japanese carriers.

The quiet competence which gained the victory at Midway caused Nimitz to select Spruance as the commander of the Fifth Fleet, the principal instrument of the Navy's Pacific offensive against Japan. Time after time Spruance struck effectively and devastatingly deep into the Japanese-controlled areas of the west-central Pacific. He wore down the Japanese navy by steady destruction of its ships and planes, while at the same time he directed and protected the island-hopping advance of Army and Marine units to the very threshold of Japan. His great victory over the Japanese navy in the Battle of the Philippine Sea was as skillful — and as decisive — as Midway. By his unprecedented feat of keeping his fleet at sea off Okinawa for more than two and a half months, under constant *Kamikaze* attack, and thousands of miles from his bases, Spruance assured the conquest of the island by Army and Marine forces.

Quiet, self-effacing, competent Spruance was the perfect example of a military professional.

Fleet Admiral William F. Halsey.
U.S. Navy Photograph

A very different kind of man was **William F. Halsey.** Not for nothing was this colorful, bold, and emotional man known as "Bull" Halsey. Nonetheless, as a naval professional he was one of the great sea dogs of all time, and unquestionably the best-known American naval hero of World War II.

Halsey was sent to the South Pacific in late 1942, when a series of naval setbacks had brought American forces to the verge of defeat and disaster on and around Guadalcanal. His boldness and determination — tempered with commendable professional caution in the face of Japanese naval superiority — soon revived the sagging morale of his command. Slowly but surely he reversed the tide at Guadalcanal, then went on to wrest control of the Solomon Islands from the Japanese in 1943. Working closely and harmoniously with General MacArthur, Halsey proved himself to be not only an inspirational naval leader and a superb administrator, but a sound and successful commander of amphibious operations.

After the successful conclusion of the South Pacific campaign, Nimitz employed Halsey and his seasoned Third Fleet staff to alternate with Spruance and the Fifth Fleet staff in operational control of Central Pacific naval forces.

Halsey's extended raids along the coasts of Japan and into the South China Sea were among the most daring exploits of naval warfare. His sound judgment in estimating the rapid decline of Japanese strength in the Philippines hastened the invasion of the Philippines by two months. His skill and his rapidly planned stratagems off Formosa led the Japanese navy into a trap which permitted him to smash, once and for all, Japanese naval air might.

Halsey's conduct of the Battle for Leyte Gulf, however, has been severely criticized. His overeagerness to destroy the Japanese navy, his failure to coordinate adequately with other naval commanders, and his stubborn refusal to change his original mistaken estimate of the situation, all caused him to fall into a Japanese trap, and came close to resulting in disaster. Nevertheless, when the battle was over — due as much to others as to himself — the Japanese navy had been decisively and disastrously defeated in the greatest naval battle of history.

Whatever one may think of Halsey's leadership at Leyte Gulf, his was one of the gigantic contributions to the Pacific victory.

Thomas C. Kinkaid was a professional peer of Spruance and Halsey. He was a cruiser division commander in the Battles of the

Admiral Thomas C. Kincaid.
Navy Department

Coral Sea and Midway, and in the early naval operations off Guadalcanal. Promoted to the command of the carrier task group after Halsey took over as South Pacific Commander, Kinkaid operated with the combination of boldness and caution which Halsey desired.

In late 1943 Kinkaid was appointed commander of the Seventh Fleet — "MacArthur's Navy." Despite the small number of vessels available to him, Kinkaid planned, conducted, and protected MacArthur's brilliant series of amphibious operations along the coast of New Guinea, in the Bismarcks, and in the Admiralties. In the process he won the complete confidence of MacArthur, and the admiration of the American, Australian, and New Zealand troops of the Southwest Pacific.

L. Admiral Marc. A. Mitscher.
Navy Department

In the Battle for Leyte Gulf, Kinkaid's fleet bore the brunt of the Japanese counterattacks, and acquitted itself brilliantly, despite difficulties of coordination with Halsey's Third Fleet. More than any other single man, Kinkaid was responsible for the overwhelming American victory in that greatest of naval battles.

The great naval aviator of World War II was Admiral **Marc A. Mitscher.** Before the war Mitscher had contributed greatly to the development of naval aviation. His defeat of Japanese naval aviation in the Solomon Islands campaign was second only to the Battle of Midway in its decisive influence on the outcome of the Pacific War.

In January, 1944, Mitscher took over the greatly expanded carrier task force of the Central Pacific Theater. This force, designated Task Force 58, was the principal striking element of Spruance's Fifth Fleet in all of its Pacific operation. Mitscher led the same force — redesignated Task Force 38 — in Halsey's Third Fleet.

Mitscher's tactical and technical conduct of carrier operations was not excelled by any naval commander of any nation. Earning the complete respect and admiration of his flyers and sailors by his professional ability, Mitscher won their love and affection by his human kindness and consideration.

The Pacific War was essentially an amphibious war. The main purpose of the fighting naval forces was to permit the conquest of Japanese-held islands in the west-central Pacific, to obtain bases from which further advances could be made. The Navy's principal expert in amphibious warfare was Admiral **Richmond K. Turner,** who directed amphibious operations first in the South Pacific, and later for Admirals Spruance and Halsey in the Central Pacific.

Turner got off to a poor start at the beginning of the Guadalcanal campaign. A force under his command was disastrously defeated at the Battle of Savo Island, and he was barely able to provide enough supplies to the Marines in the early days after the landing. Nevertheless, "Kelly" Turner's ingenuity, determination, and administrative skill were recognized by both Nimitz and Halsey. Thus Turner got another chance to show what he could do — and it was close to perfection.

There were many other Pacific naval commanders who deserve favorable comment and consideration. For instance, Admirals **Theodore S. Wilkinson** and **Daniel E. Barbey** were both worthy students of Turner. And the early war operations of Admirals **Thomas C. Hart** and **Frank Jack Fletcher** were commendable, particularly since they both fought against a much more powerful enemy. But space does not permit further consideration of other naval commanders, while the professional limitations of the author do not permit valid assessments of lesser-known tactical and technical naval accomplishments.

SAILORS OF THE ATLANTIC AND MEDITERRANEAN

The Navy played a much less dominant role in the war against the European Axis than it did in the Pacific. Yet what it did was absolutely vital — even if relatively thankless. In the first place, the Navy eliminated the submarine menace in the long-drawn-out Battle of the Atlantic; secondly, it moved Army forces to the beaches, then supported them with firepower, in the major amphibious landings on the coasts of North Africa and Western Europe.

The man who exercised overall responsibility for the conduct of these two important missions during most of the war was Admiral **Royal E. Ingersoll.** He commanded the Atlantic Fleet from January, 1942, until November, 1944. Thus, to him must go the credit for the decisive Allied victory against German submarines in the Battle of the Atlantic. He also had responsibility for the conducting of all troop convoys to Europe and for supervising all of the major amphibious operations of the European war. He was succeeded by Admiral **Jonas H. Ingram,** who had been one of Ingersoll's most capable subordinates in the antisubmarine and troop convoy missions. Ingram continued in command of the Atlantic Fleet until after the end of the war.

The principal amphibious operational commanders in European and African waters were Admirals **Henry K. Hewitt,** and **Alan G. Kirk.** Hewitt, who had been one of the Navy's principal amphibious specialists, commanded the naval support forces for the Moroccan landings in the fall of 1942, and led the American elements of all subsequent Mediterranean landing operations: Sicily, Salerno, and southern France. Kirk, who had been one of Hewitt's principal subordinates before the war, and then in the Mediterranean operations, was shifted to England in 1944 to become the commander of American naval forces in the Normandy invasion.

The technical ability of these two naval officers was certainly comparable to that of Kelly Turner in the Pacific. And they had a problem which never bothered Turner: they had to get along with skeptical and imperious British naval officers who found it difficult to realize that American naval men could fight as well as the Royal Navy. It is to the credit of Hewitt and Kirk — and also to their British counterparts — that Allied naval relations were never seriously strained.

THE MARINES

United States Marines have always had a reputation as tough, resourceful, hard-bitten, fighting men. In the Pacific War this reputation was reinforced and the traditions of the Corps enriched by the performance of Marine commanders at all levels, from squad to corps. Because the Marines always operated under the overall command of the Navy — and sometimes under intermediate

Army commanders — there was no opportunity for any Marine to exercise independent command of any operation larger than that of a corps, nor for any period of time beyond a few weeks, or, at most, months.

Marine casualties in the Pacific War were substantially greater than those of comparable Army units, on any basis of comparison. There are several reasons for this. First was the fact that almost invariably the Marines were employed by the Navy to seize small, intensively fortified and fanatically defended Japanese-held island bases. There was no opportunity for strategic and tactical surprise, and little possibility of maneuver. Such positions could be taken only at the cost of severe sacrifices by superbly trained and disciplined troops under vigorous, determined commanders. The Marines were invariably successful in such operations.

There was another reason for these heavy casualties which reflects credit upon Marine traditions, but which was questioned seriously by some of the Army commanders who fought beside them. Rightly priding themselves and their troops as tough fighting men, and ever aware of the fleeting nature of time, Marine commanders would sometimes disdain to take the time to try tactical maneuvers, or to allow supporting arms to soften the foe with high-explosive bombardment. They simply smashed their way through Japanese defenses in frontal assaults that unquestionably saved precious time — but which also lost precious lives.

The man who achieved the most widespread reputation for this kind of vigorous, costly, and time-saving assault was **Holland M. Smith.** He was known far and wide as "Howlin' Mad" Smith, both because of the intensity and thoroughness of his training program, and because of his apparent disregard for casualties in combat.

General Holland M. Smith.
Defense Department Photo

Smith was overall commander of ground assault operations in the Gilberts, the Marshalls, the Marianas, and at Iwo Jima.

Perhaps the most explosive controversy of the war involved Smith, then a lieutenant general commanding the V Amphibious Corps in the invasion of Saipan, and Army Major General Ralph C. Smith, commanding the Army's 27th Infantry Division as part of that corps. Marine General H. M. Smith was not satisfied with the performance of Army General R. C. Smith and his division, because they were not moving fast enough, and because they were not taking enough casualties. When Army General Smith showed his resentment, "Howlin' Mad" simply relieved him of his command. A subsequent Army investigation reported that Army General Smith had exercised sound judgment and good leadership, but "Howlin' Mad" still insisted that he had been right.

In fact, the incident proved nothing, other than the fact that Marine commanders, geared to sharp, intensive combat, are willing to take heavier casualties than most Army commanders in fighting to gain their objectives.

The Marine who became best known to the American public was **Alexander A. Vandegrift,** who commanded the 1st Marine Division on Guadalcanal. In the early days of that campaign Vandegrift and his tough division were almost completely isolated, since the Japanese had regained control of the sea and of the air around Guadalcanal shortly after the American landing. The fortitude, determination, and fighting qualities of Vandegrift and his men under these dismaying conditions were representative of the very finest traditions of the U.S. Marine Corps. It is impossible to give higher praise to soldiers.

American Air Force Commanders

With two or three exceptions, the principal combat airmen of World War II did not make as much of an impression upon the public, or upon historians, as did the soldiers and sailors. Air commanders could not (for the most part) influence the outcome of air battles so directly nor so personally as could ground and naval commanders. Furthermore, air commanders had little opportunity to make vital, war-changing decisions. Operations of the strategic air forces were closely controlled by the Combined and Joint Chiefs of Staff; operations of the tactical air forces were generally geared to those of ground and naval forces.

Major General Claire L. Chennault.

Yet, because of their personalities, or the special situations in which they found themselves, a few of the senior airmen of World War II caught public interest and attention.

Claire L. Chennault was probably the most brilliant aerial tactician of World War II. He was also one of the most controversial figures of the war.

In 1937 Chennault had retired from the United States Army Air Corps because he was slightly deaf; he had reached the rank of major, after twenty years of military service, was recognized as an excellent tactician, but was equally noted for his lack of tact, and for his interest in new and untried tactical concepts. After his retirement Chennault went to China to become Chiang Kai-shek's

41

principal adviser on aeronautical affairs. In 1941 he established the American mercenary air group known to history as the Flying Tigers. In spectacular victories over more numerous Japanese air units, Chennault proved the efficacy of his new tactical concepts, and also proved himself a superb leader of men.

During most of the following three years Chennault was engaged in controversy with his immediate superior officer, General "Joe" Stilwell. Chennault, believing that a small but highly efficient air force could drive the Japanese from China, felt that all of the limited cargo space available in the "Hump" airlift to isolated China should go to his air force. Stilwell believed that this airlift capacity should be shared between the air force and the Chinese army, in order to permit the development of a balanced air and ground combat capability.

When overruled by Stilwell, Chennault, in some devious politicking, went behind Stilwell's back. With the help of Generalissimo Chiang, he obtained the personal support of President Roosevelt. Stilwell was forced to let Chennault have the cargo space he had demanded.

The climax of the controversy came in 1944 when the Japanese army almost overwhelmed China, despite the best efforts of Chennault and an air force considerably larger than that with which he had earlier promised to defeat the Japanese.

For all of his unparalleled tactical genius, crusty Claire Chennault never fully understood either the limitations of air power, or the vital importance of coordination of all elements of military force in war.

James H. Doolittle was another former Regular Army Air Corps officer. Generally hailed as the finest — and fastest — pilot in the

*Lieutenant General
James H. Doolittle.*

United States, Doolittle had resigned in 1930 in order to enter business, and also to set new world speed records as a private flyer. He was also one of the very first pilots to experiment with, and to help develop, "blind flying," with instruments only.

Doolittle came dramatically to the attention of the American public in April, 1942, as leader of the valiant carrier-borne air raid against Japan, when morale in the United States was at its lowest ebb. He was awarded the Medal of Honor for this feat, which also started his meteoric rise from lieutenant colonel to major general in eight months.

Though he had begun his air career as a fighter pilot, Doolittle was a long-range bomber commander throughout the remainder of

World War II. He was placed in command of the newly created Twelfth Air Force in North Africa in early 1943, and then took command of the Fifteenth Air Force when that was established in Italy after the successful landings at Salerno. Early in 1944 he was transferred to England, where he took command of the Army Air Force's oldest and best-known bombardment unit: the Eighth Air Force. After the defeat of Germany he led the Eighth Air Force to Okinawa, where it briefly participated in the final air assaults against Japan.

Doolittle was one of the most versatile airmen in the brief history of air power. No one contributed more than he personally did to the development of air-mindedness in the United States; no commander proved himself more efficient or more courageous in combat.

Although still a relatively junior major general at the close of World War II, **Curtis E. LeMay** had attracted such attention in military circles by his brilliance as a commander of the B-29 Superfortresses that his scowling face and ever-present cigar were already well known to the American public.

LeMay was as outstanding in the development of bombardment tactics as Chennault had been in fighter tactics. Interestingly, the two men worked closely together for a few months in 1944, when LeMay's XX Bomber Command of long-range Superfortresses cooperated with Chennault's Fourteenth Air Force over northern and eastern China. Later, when he was operating from Saipan, LeMay's most successful tactical innovation — the low-level incendiary raids on Japan — was in large part inspired by suggestions he had received from Chennault in a raid against Hankow in December, 1944.

General Curtis E. Le-May.

LeMay had first shown his great tactical ability as an air commander under Spaatz and Eaker in the Eighth Air Force, from late 1942 to early 1944. It was this ability which led to his selection as leader of the XX Bomber Command, when the first Superforts were sent to India and China. His success there, and later with the XXI Bomber Command in the Marianas, led directly to his postwar selection as commander of America's Strategic Air Command.

LeMay's principal mentor during World War II was America's senior combat airman: **Carl Spaatz.** Spaatz was one of the few World War II airmen who had fought in aerial combat in World

General Carl Spaatz.

War I, when he had earned the Distinguished Service Cross. He was the first commander of the Eighth Air Force, in Britain, in 1942–43, then took command of all air operations in North Africa in 1943. Early in 1944 he returned to England to become the first commander of the U.S. Strategic Air Force, which included the Eighth Air Force and the Fifteenth Air Force in Italy.

For approximately a year and a half, under the direction of the Combined Chiefs of Staff, Spaatz commanded the American effort in the great strategic bombing assault against Germany. Then, with Germany defeated, Spaatz moved his headquarters to the Mariana Islands, in the Pacific, where he directed the final phases of the American strategic bombardment of Japan.

"Toohey" Spaatz became the first Chief of Staff of the United States Air Force, when it was established by the National Defense Act of 1947. Quiet, calm, self-effacing so far as the public was concerned, Spaatz was a superb example of military professionalism to the officers of the newly created service.

Closely associated with Spaatz in the strategic offensives against Germany was **Ira C. Eaker.** When the Eighth Air Force was established under Spaatz, in 1942, Eaker was the senior division commander, and led the first American bombing operation against Western Europe, in August, 1942. When Spaatz moved to North Africa, Eaker took command of the Eighth Air Force and directed its great expansion during 1943.

Early in 1944 Eaker was transferred to the Mediterranean Theater of Operations, where he was placed in command of the Mediterranean Allied Air Forces — with the Fifteenth Air Force as his principal combat unit. He retained this position until the end of the war.

Outstanding among the competent tactical air force commanders in Europe in World War II was **Hoyt S. Vandenberg.** After serving under Spaatz and Doolittle as the Chief of Staff of the Twelfth Air Force, in August, 1944, Vandenberg took command of the Ninth Air Force, the American contingent of the Allied Expeditionary Air Force of General Eisenhower's vast command. He retained this post until the end of the war, directing and coordinating the tactical air support given to all of the American armies in northwestern Europe.

General Hoyt S. Van-denberg.

In the war against Japan, **George C. Kenney** was the dominant Army Air Force commander. Like Spaatz, he had had a distinguished record as a combat pilot in the U.S. Army Air Service in World War I. In July, 1942, he was placed in command of Allied Air Forces in the Southwest Pacific Theater, under General Mac-Arthur. He retained this position until the end of the war, commanding the Fifth Air Force, and then the Far East Air Forces — which included both the Fifth and Thirteenth Air Forces.

Kenney — a small, intense, peppery man — was an imaginative and daring commander who earned the respect and admiration of General MacArthur and of all of the ground commanders in the Southwest Pacific Theater. He and his staff developed the highly

General George C. Kenney.

efficient pattern of tactical air support operations which proved so successful in that theater. Kenney devoted much attention to the development of new and effective methods of low-level bombing. The skip-bombing technique which proved so effective in the Battle of the Bismarck Sea was originated by him, and he personally spent much time in improving such techniques and in supervising the incessant training required to make them effective.

British Army Commanders in the Field

No MAN better represented the strengths and weaknesses of the British army at the outset of World War II than did General Lord **John Vereker,** 6th **Viscount Gort.** After having been Chief of the Imperial General Staff from 1937 to 1939, he was placed in command of the British Expeditionary Force — or BEF — in France soon after war began.

Gort had demonstrated great courage in World War I, and had risen early to senior rank between the wars. But in the process he had had little chance to command troops, and had not kept abreast of modern military developments. To the despair of his two principal subordinates, Generals John Dill and Alan Brooke,* Gort obviously expected World War II to follow the same tactical patterns as had the previous war. He was relatively unconcerned about shortages of modern weapons and equipment. And worst of all, Dill and Brooke thought, Gort did not recognize the potentially fatal weaknesses in the French army, and tied his own army to outdated French methods of warfare.

When the German invasion smashed the French plans in May, 1940, Gort fought courageously, and withdrew toward the English Channel trying to keep his army intact. But for a while he was confused because of the collapse of French and Belgian armies on his flanks, and because of his own inability to react to German *blitzkrieg* tactics. That his withdrawal to Dunkirk was accomplished with amazing success was due primarily to the coolness and professional skill of General Brooke, commanding the II Corps.

Gort never had another chance for field command in battle. His courage and cheerfulness under adversity served his nation well, however, when he was later commander of Malta during its long months under constant Axis air attacks.

Least known of the truly great leaders of World War II was Field Marshal **Archibald P. Wavell.** As a young officer in World War I, he had served closely under Allenby in Palestine and was

*Both of these men are included among British strategic leaders, in Volume 18 of this series.

Field Marshal Archibald P. Wavell (right) in Singapore.
Imperial War Museum

greatly influenced by Britain's most successful soldier of the earlier war.

In July, 1939, Wavell was appointed Commander in Chief of the Middle East Command, which included Egypt, the Sudan, East Africa, Palestine, and Iraq. The most spectacular victories of World War II were those which his forces — under the field command of able young General **Richard N. O'Connor** in Libya and General Sir **Alan Cunningham** in East Africa — gained against enormous odds over the Italians in late 1940 and early 1941.

Before Wavell could consolidate these victories by overrunning all of Libya, he was ordered to send an expeditionary force to Greece, only to see this small force overwhelmed during the German invasion of the Balkans. At this same time he had to fight the Vichy-French in Syria, and to suppress a German-supported uprising in Iraq. Wavell had strongly protested against sending troops to Greece, but Churchill felt that Britain's political obligations demanded the risk. After the disaster in Greece, Churchill seems to have wrongly suspected Wavell of saying "I told you so" when he requested reinforcements to meet a new German buildup in Libya under German General Rommel.

Because of that buildup, Rommel quickly reconquered the portions of Libya that the British had taken a few months earlier. Despite a continuing shortage of troops, Wavell obeyed the Prime Minister's demand for a counteroffensive, and was badly repulsed. Churchill did not recognize that the succession of defeats in Greece, Crete, and Libya had been the result of Wavell's obedience to his, Churchill's, own orders, and so the Prime Minister relieved the unfortunate general from command and sent him to India. In his attitude toward Wavell, Churchill displayed his most serious human weakness.

When the Pacific War began, Wavell was placed in command of the so-called ABDA (American-British-Dutch-Australian) forces trying to stop the Japanese drive into Southeast Asia and the East Indies. In fact, however, he had no chance to coordinate or control these far-flung units, which were quickly defeated, one at a time, by the Japanese. Churchill again blamed Wavell for the disasters, particularly for the British defeats in Malaya, Singapore, and Burma. Soon afterward Wavell was appointed Viceroy of India, and General Auchinleck was appointed Commander in Chief, India, in his place.

Unfortunately for Wavell's fame, much of what he accomplished in Libya had to be done again, and so he is perhaps best known for his failures. His victories, however, combined with the resourcefulness and determination which he showed in adversity, are enough to merit Wavell a place of honor amongst the handful of Britain's greatest generals.

One British general who successfully exercised high command during the war was never well known to the public: **Henry M. Wilson.** A big, heavy man, "Jumbo" Wilson shared with Wavell and O'Connor credit for the great victory over the Italians in Libya in 1940. He also led the ill-fated expeditionary force to Greece, and then commanded the little army that won Syria from the Vichy-French in the summer of 1941. He remained in the Middle East as commander of the Ninth Army after Wavell was replaced by Auchinleck, then in the summer of 1942 was placed in command of forces in Persia and Iraq, to prepare to meet the threatened German drive through the Caucasus. Early in 1943 he followed General Alexander as Middle East Commander, and then took over the Mediterranean Command from Eisenhower in January, 1944. A year later he was appointed British Chiefs of Staff representative in Washington, following the death of Field Marshal Dill. A competent, reliable professional, Wilson performed well all the tasks he was given, but never displayed the imagination or brilliance of a great captain.

Field Marshal Bernard L. Montgomery greeted by the author (right) at Boston Airport, 1956.

The best-known British general of World War II was **Bernard L. Montgomery.** "Monty" was not the greatest general of World War II (as he probably believed), nor was he even the best British general of the war. He was, however, a consistently successful commander from start to finish. He led a division in the ill-fated British Expeditionary Force in France, being one of the few generals who came out of that disaster with his reputation improved. He was also a remarkably lucky general, but more than luck is needed for consistent battlefield success, even when the tides of war are favorable.

Montgomery's greatest stroke of luck was in being named commander of the British Eighth Army at the time it was beginning to be greatly reinforced and provided with plentiful supplies from America — just when Rommel's supply line was beginning to run dry. His second stroke of luck was in being placed under the command of a quiet, self-effacing man like General Alexander, who did not interfere with subordinates who performed well. But these strokes of luck would have been to no avail if Montgomery had not seized upon the situation to rebuild the shattered morale of the Eighth Army, to prepare it meticulously for combat, to impress his personality upon the men, and to prepare his first battle plan on the basis of a shrewd and carefully studied estimate of where and how Rommel would strike next.

Analysis of Montgomery's first battle in command of the Eighth Army — Alam el Halfa — reveals both his greatness and his weakness as a general. The preparations were perfect; he laid a trap for Rommel which the German could not avoid, and which the Afrika Korps was too weak to break. As Montgomery expected, it was a defensive success which breathed new confidence into the Eighth Army — confidence in itself and confidence in this shrewd, colorful leader who gave them the victory he had promised in the fashion he had promised.

The victory, however, had hurt Rommel's Afrika Korps more grievously than Montgomery had anticipated. A truly great general would have seized this opportunity to improvise new orders, and to pursue; the Afrika Korps could have been smashed. Of course, the improvised plans could have miscarried, and wily Rommel could have counterattacked. With this in mind, Montgomery did not pursue; it was not in his plan. He was completely satisfied to do just what he had set out to do, and no more.

When he finally did smash the Afrika Korps — after the long and costly Battle of El Alamein — Montgomery was ready to pursue, and pursue he did, for more than 2,000 miles. It was an efficient, well-conducted operation — Montgomery's always were. Americans have criticized Monty's insistence on "tidy" operations; they say he never attacked until he had so much strength that success was inevitable; they have accused him of being overcautious.

The American critics were wrong. Montgomery impressed upon his soldiers the fact that he always made every possible effort to win his battles with the least possible loss of life. As a result, morale was always high in Monty's armies. He was cautious, he was bombastic, he was egotistical — and he was successful. The payoff is on the final score.

Harold R. L. G. Alexander was a typical Guards Officer. No matter how difficult or how dangerous a situation might be, no matter how much excitement or enthusiasm there might be around him, Alexander was always cool, calm, and quiet. In the retreat to Dunkirk he was a division commander. General Brooke wrote in his diary: "Alex . . . gave me the impression of never realizing all the unpleasant potentialities of our predicament. He remained entirely unaffected by it, completely composed, and appeared never to have the slightest doubt that all would come right in the end."

A few nights later — just before midnight on June 2, 1940 — Alexander gave a similar impression to the few officers and men who were with him as he checked the beaches of Dunkirk on foot and in a motorboat. He had been appointed commander of the British rear guard, and he wished to be sure that all his men were embarked. Not till then did he go aboard a destroyer to return to England.

Field Marshal Sir Harold R. L. G. Alexander.
U.S. Army Photograph

Less than two years later in Burma he gave that same impression to the officers, soldiers, and civilians around him when they discovered (three days after he had arrived) that the Japanese had blocked the only escape route from Rangoon. Calmly Alexander dealt with the situation and, taking advantage of a temporary Japanese lapse, slipped out of the trap.

The record of his accomplishments is clear evidence that underneath Alexander's imperturbable exterior lay a brilliant military intellect, firm determination, and a sharply aggressive offensive spirit.

The Burma campaign had been a disaster when Alexander took command; it concluded as a bitter Allied defeat. But Alexander — with magnificent assistance from Generals Stilwell and Slim — succeeded in pulling out most of the British, Indian, and Chinese forces. Following this he was selected by Churchill and Brooke to replace General Auchinleck as Commander in Chief of the Middle East Command. With his usual calm, quiet, self-effacing efficiency he built up the force of which Montgomery's Eighth Army was the spearhead. Typically, he permitted his subordinate, Monty, to gain all of the public acclaim which followed the victory of Alexander's Middle East Command over Rommel in Egypt and Libya.

As the Germans were squeezed into Tunisia, Alexander was appointed Deputy Supreme Commander, Mediterranean, under Eisenhower, and became the field force commander for the Tunisian campaign.

Under Eisenhower's overall command, Alexander remained in command of the ground operations in the Mediterranean for the invasions of Sicily and Italy. He commanded field operations in Italy for the remainder of 1943 and all of 1944, being promoted to Supreme Commander of the Mediterranean Theater early in 1945. In this post he received the surrender of all of the Germans in Italy and in the Balkans in May, 1945.

Unquestionably Alexander was one of the most capable British generals of World War II.

The reputations of many fine British officers were ruined or tarnished on the Western Desert between Egypt and Libya, and mostly at the hands of the German Rommel. Next, perhaps, to Wavell's misfortunes, the most tragic were those of General **Claude J. E. Auchinleck.** "The Auk," as he was known, had served with distinction in World War I. Between the wars his service had been outstanding in India. He had commanded the Narvik expedition in 1940, the one successful Allied operation in Norway, but was forced to withdraw because of the disasters in Flanders and France. Soon afterward he was appointed Commander in Chief, India, but he had been there barely six months before he succeeded Wavell as Commander in Chief, Middle East, in July, 1941.

Energetically and competéntly he reorganized the Western Desert Force, which was rechristened the Eighth Army in October. Immediate commander of the Eighth Army was General Alan Cunningham, who had conquered East Africa under Wavell.

In mid-November, Auchinleck directed a major attack against Rommel; when the Eighth Army faltered, he took personal command of the battle, and in a six-week lightning campaign drove Rommel out of Cyrenaica. But Rommel quickly regrouped, and counterattacked in January. He drove the Eighth Army halfway back across Cyrenaica before Auchinleck, assisted by General **Neil Ritchie,** stopped the Germans near El Gazala. A few months later Rommel again struck and inflicted a disastrous defeat on the Eighth Army in a long, bitter battle near El Gazala. Rommel pursued vigorously into Egypt, and got within 60 miles of Alexandria before Auchinleck — again taking over personal control of the land battle — stopped him at El Alamein in July, 1942.

Although Churchill and Brooke recognized the personal brilliance and skill which Auchinleck had displayed, they also realized that the morale of his army was shattered, and that he had lost the confidence of his officers and men. Auchinleck, bitterly disappointed, was replaced by Alexander, and Montgomery took over the Eighth Army. Auchinleck never again had a chance to display his professional competence in combat.

Field Marshal Sir William Slim.
Imperial War Museum

A real soldier's soldier was **William Joseph Slim.** He enlisted as a private in World War I; he commanded a victorious army at the close of World War II, and was promoted to field marshal. He has written the best military memoirs of World War II. And, perhaps the greatest achievement of all, he was the only "Limey" — Englishman — that crusty General Joe Stilwell was proud to call a friend.

Slim commanded a brigade in the conquest of East Africa in 1940–41; after a brief tour on the Western Desert, he commanded a division in the pacification of Iraq and northern Iran in 1941. This success led to his appointment as commander of the battered Burma Corps shortly after the Japanese invasion of Burma in early 1942.

With the assistance and support of General Alexander, Slim reorganized and revitalized the Burma Corps during the bitter fighting of the spring of 1942 in south-central Burma. Here he first met — and liked — "Vinegar Joe" Stilwell, whose Chinese Expeditionary Force was fighting beside his corps. Stilwell found Slim to be a soldier of the same vigor, imagination, and integrity that he was himself. Though both generals were bitterly disappointed by their defeat in Burma that year, both knew they had done their best, and that between them they had saved many thousands of fine Allied soldiers who would otherwise have been killed or captured by the Japanese.

Like Stilwell, Slim had a chance to fight his way back to Burma. As commander of the Fourteenth Army he first repulsed a Japanese invasion of India, then counterattacked, to conquer central and southern Burma in one of the most perfectly planned and executed campaigns of World War II. Particularly brilliant was the plan — as well as the execution — of his bold turning movement across the Irrawaddy River, in which he cut the lines of communication between the main Japanese army, near Mandalay, and its base at Rangoon.

A splendid administrator; an inspiring leader of men; brilliant strategist and tactician; determined, courageous professional fighting man in defeat and in victory; "Bill" Slim was unquestionably one of the great soldiers of World War II.

61

There were many other splendid British generals who proved their competence and who typified the toughness of their island breed in the greatest of all wars. But we cannot note them all. Some, like O'Connor, captured in the Western Desert, suffered from the fortunes of war without a chance to fully reveal great promise. This was true also of the Dominion generals like New Zealand's **Freyberg** and Australia's **Blamey,** who always served under Englishmen or Americans. Others, like **Crerar** and **Dempsey,** were outshone by the brilliance of their commander. A few, like **Wingate,** were perhaps overrated.

Royal Navy Commanders at Sea

FOR REASONS which baffle the historian, the Royal Navy has fought and won some of its most desperate struggles against opponents who had better and faster ships — and sometimes had more of them. This was true in World War II.

In actual numbers the British had a slight superiority over the combined German and Italian fleets after the surrender of France, in 1940. But the requirements of protecting vital supply convoys from the submarine menace, plus the necessity for retaining naval forces to protect British coasts against possible German invasion, gave the Germans several opportunities to raid into the Atlantic with warships bigger and faster than any the British had. At the same time, the German submarine fleet not only took a heavy toll of British warships, but came very close to isolating and starving Britain.

In the Mediterranean the Italians not only had more warships throughout the early years of the war, but there was a period in late 1941 and early 1942 when Italian superiority was so over-

Admiral of the Fleet Sir Andrew B. Cunningham.
Office of Chief of Naval Operations

whelming that it seemed that only a miracle could prevent the pitiful remnants of the British Mediterranean Fleet from being overwhelmed. A similar situation existed against the Japanese in the Indian Ocean at almost the same time.

But although the Royal Navy has sometimes found it difficult to match the ships of an opponent, it has never been inferior in the seamanship, courage, or fighting ability of its men.

In the Mediterranean, for instance, in the dismal winter of 1941–42, the Royal Navy did not really need a miracle; it had Admiral **Andrew B. Cunningham.*** Having entered the navy at the age of fifteen, Cunningham served through World War I, and had risen to command the Mediterranean Fleet at the outset of World

---

* Brother of General Alan Cunningham.

War II. Cunningham seized the initiative, and by several bold sweeps close to the Italian coast, gained a complete moral ascendancy over the larger and more powerful Italian navy. In an early engagement off Calabria, Cunningham in his flagship — the battleship HMS *Warspite* — boldly engaged two Italian battleships, with double his own firepower. The Italian admiral — who was supported by twice as many cruisers and destroyers — refused to accept the challenge, and by virtue of the greater speed of his ships soon got out of Cunningham's range.

Unable to get the Italians to come out to fight, Cunningham in November, 1940, carried out a bold naval air raid against the Italian fleet in Taranto Harbor. This success briefly brought the two fleets close to numerical equality in major warships, but repairs and new construction enabled the Italians to regain superiority by March, 1941. By this time Cunningham's fleet was busily engaged in convoying the British Expeditionary Force to Greece.

Taking advantage of this situation, the Italian fleet ventured out into the Ionian Sea. Cunningham, who had been hoping for this, was ready. While a few small British ships enticed the Italians into a chase near Cape Matapan, Cunningham's main fleet dashed to engage the more numerous enemy. Warned by reconnaissance aircraft just in time to avoid a full-scale engagement, the Italians again fled, but this time suffered considerable damage before their greater speed again got them out of range.

Then came the Battles of Greece and of Crete, with Cunningham's fleet engaged in rescuing the remnants of two British expeditionary forces, while fighting incessant battles against the German air force. British losses were so severe that Churchill felt that no more vessels or sailors should be risked in the waters around Crete.

But Cunningham radioed to all of his ships: "Stick it out. We must never let the Army down." And they didn't!

These British losses gave the Italian navy about a two-to-one superiority in the Mediterranean — but they no longer dared to risk battle with Cunningham.

Disaster struck the British in November and December, 1941. First a German submarine sank Cunningham's only carrier. On December 19 explosive charges placed by six courageous Italian frogmen blasted great holes in the hulls of two of his three battle-ships, putting them out of action for months. That same day a cruiser and a destroyer were sunk in a minefield laid by a German submarine, and two other cruisers were so badly damaged as to be put out of action indefinitely. Six days later — Christmas — Cunningham's last battleship was sunk by a German submarine; the following day another cruiser was sent to the bottom by a U-boat.

Cunningham was left with a handful of cruisers and destroyers. Boldly he sent these vessels out to sea in a desperate bluff against the overwhelmingly superior Italian navy. The Italians stayed in port, and this tiny British fleet still controlled the surface of the Mediterranean.

Less than two years later, in September, 1943, Cunningham's rebuilt fleet escorted the surrendering Italian navy to Malta, and he sent his famous message to the Admiralty: "Be pleased to inform their Lordships that the Italian battle fleet now lies at anchor under the guns of the fortress of Malta." A month later the death of Admiral Pound led to Cunningham's appointment as First Sea Lord; he kept this post to the end of the war.

Cunningham's name will deservedly take a place of honor beside predecessors like Drake, Blake, Jervis, and Nelson.

Admiral Sir **Bruce Fraser** was Third Sea Lord in the Admiralty in London for the first three years of the war. Early in 1943 he took command of the British Home Fleet. His principal concerns were the powerful German battleships *Tirpitz* and *Scharnhorst*, both based in northern Norway, and both dangerous threats to Allied convoys in the North Atlantic and Arctic oceans. During the following months Fraser, cruising in the North Atlantic on his flagship, the battleship HMS *Duke of York*, vainly tried to entice the German ships into battle. Then, on Christmas Eve, 1943, intercepted German messages revealed to the British that the *Scharnhorst* was at sea, stalking an Allied convoy to Murmansk. Fraser, who was steaming east of Iceland, ordered a nearby cruiser squadron to engage the *Scharnhorst* while he raced to join the action.

Early on December 26, Fraser's *Duke of York* joined the cruisers, already engaged in a running fight with the *Scharnhorst*. At extreme range the British battleship scored hits, crippling the German warship just before her superior speed would have pulled her out of range. In the ensuing battle the *Scharnhorst* was sunk.

Fraser never had a chance to fight the giant *Tirpitz* on the open sea. But between his carrier planes and long-range RAF bombers, the giant German battleship was severely damaged, and eventually was sunk at her moorings, in November, 1944. Meanwhile, Fraser had in August taken over the Indian Ocean Fleet, which in November became the British Pacific Fleet. He retained this command until the end of the war, working closely and cordially with Admirals Nimitz and Spruance, and with General MacArthur.

Fraser was a fighting admiral, a sea dog in the finest tradition of the Royal Navy.

Another such was Admiral **James F. Somerville.** Retired from active service in 1939, due to ill health, after having commanded the East Indies Fleet, he volunteered to return to active duty upon the outbreak of the war. In late June he was assigned one of the most distasteful tasks ever given a British admiral.

When France surrendered in 1940, the thinly stretched Royal Navy had to take over the responsibility for securing the western Mediterranean, a task which the French navy had been performing. Somerville was sent to Gibraltar with a force consisting of two battleships, a battle cruiser, an aircraft carrier, and several cruisers and destroyers.

Somerville was directed to proceed to Mers-el-Kebir, the French naval base near Oran, in Algeria, where there were four French battleships and a number of destroyers. He was ordered to give the French commander three choices: joining the British fleet in carrying on the war against Germany; demilitarizing the French warships in a British port, an overseas French port, or in the United States; or sinking his ships in Mers-el-Kebir. If the French did not agree to one of these alternatives, Somerville was to use whatever force was necessary to put the French ships out of action.

On July 3, 1940, the French admiral refused the three alternatives. Since French naval reinforcements were approaching from Toulon and Algiers, Somerville opened fire against his former allies. Although the French vessels had been prepared for action, they were quickly defeated by the British. Three of the French battleships were sunk or beached; the fourth escaped to Toulon.

In subsequent months Somerville operated in the western Mediterranean and eastern Atlantic, cooperating closely with Cunningham's Mediterranean Fleet. It was his aircraft carrier, HMS *Ark Royal*, which struck the crippling blows against the giant *Bismarck*;

67

Admiral of the Fleet Sir James F. Somerville.
U.S. Army Photograph

to him were entrusted the important Malta convoys in the fall of 1941.

In March, 1942, Somerville was sent to the Indian Ocean, arriving to take command of the British fleet there just as Admiral Nagumo's victorious Japanese First Air Fleet swept into the Indian Ocean. Somerville's fleet was far weaker than that of the Japanese, but with typical Royal Navy aggressiveness he sailed out to meet them. It was probably fortunate for the British that the two fleets passed each other without making contact. Later, under orders from the Admiralty, Somerville sent his old and slow ships back to the coast of East Africa, but continued to harass the Japanese in the eastern Indian Ocean with the few modern vessels available to him.

By 1944 the progress of the war in Europe was such that Somerville received substantial reinforcements and was able to take the offensive against Japanese sea-lanes and installations in the eastern Indian Ocean. He struck with carrier forces against Sumatra and

Java; he completely severed the Japanese sea route from Singapore to Rangoon.

His health still poor, Somerville was relieved from his arduous duties in August, 1944, by Admiral Fraser. He spent the remainder of the war at the head of the British naval delegation in Washington, where he upheld the honor of the Royal Navy as well as he had done at sea.

Like Somerville, Admiral Sir **Bertram H. Ramsay** had retired from active duty before the war. The outbreak of hostilities, however, caused him to be brought back to service, and he was appointed Flag Officer, Dover. Thus, in May, 1940, Churchill entrusted to him the execution of "Operation Dynamo." This was the tremendous, improvised mission of evacuating British and Allied troops from the beaches of Dunkirk. There could be no greater tribute than the notes which General Brooke later wrote in his diary when he learned that Ramsay was directing the operations:

> I still have the most vivid recollection of the wonderful relief of finding a man of Ramsay's caliber handling the difficult situation. I know of no other sailor whom I would sooner have seen responsible for extricating my old corps and the BEF.

When he ordered the operation Churchill had hoped that perhaps 50,000 men might be rescued. When the operation ended, on June 4, 1940, Ramsay and his sailors had evacuated 224,000 British troops, plus another 142,000 French and Belgian soldiers. It was called "the miracle of Dunkirk" by the British people; as so often in British history, behind the miracle was a bluff, determined admiral of the Royal Navy.

Admiral Sir Bertram H. Ramsay.
Office of War Information

Later, Ramsay commanded the naval task force which convoyed and supported the landing of Montgomery's Eighth Army in Sicily, and then on the shores of Italy. The following year came his greatest mission: command of the naval forces for the invasion of Normandy. Ramsay controlled and directed his 5,000 vessels with customary skill and efficiency; much of the success of "Operation Overlord" was due to his practiced, professional competence.

It is a tribute both to Ramsay and to Eisenhower that in their cooperation in the invasion was formed one of the great friendships of the war. Ramsay remained one of Eisenhower's closest and most trusted advisers — on one occasion even arguing with Eisenhower against Churchill in support of American strategic views. It was a tragedy to the Allies, and a great personal loss to Eisenhower, when Ramsay was killed in an air crash near Paris, in January, 1945.

Youngest and most glamorous of Britain's senior naval officers in World War II was Admiral Lord **Louis Mountbatten.** The fact that he was a cousin of the King did not hurt him in his rise to high command; but he got to the top on merit.

Mountbatten entered the navy as a midshipman at the age of thirteen, and saw action in World War I. In the early days of World War II he distinguished himself as a bold and resolute destroyer commander. He gained particular fame in the Battle of Crete, where his ship was sunk in a desperate battle with German planes. He was rescued, and later briefly commanded the aircraft carrier HMS *Illustrious.* In late 1941 he replaced elderly Admiral Sir Roger Keyes in command of Combined Operations — the British Commando headquarters. He retained this post, where he exercised great influence on Churchill, for nearly two years, and was responsible for training and directing the Commandos, whose operations caused the Germans so many headaches. He must also bear some responsibility for the tragic failure of the Allied raid at Dieppe, in August, 1942, as well as for the successful British invasion of Madagascar later that year.

In August, 1943, at the Quebec Conference, the Combined Chiefs of Staff agreed to establish an Allied Southeast Asia Command, with Mountbatten as Supreme Commander. The main rea-

Admiral of the Fleet Lord Louis Mountbatten
U.S. Army Photograph

son for his appointment was the expectation that a major share of the operations in this theater would be amphibious assaults against the coasts of Burma, Malaya, Sumatra, and Singapore. This was not to be; resources in landing craft and supporting warships were not great enough to permit such operations when requirements were more urgent in Europe and the Pacific. So, save for a few minor coastal operations, Admiral Mountbatten commanded an entirely overland campaign.

The principal battlefield commanders in this campaign, as we have seen, were those staunch soldiers, Slim and Stilwell. They were ably supported, however, by Mountbatten, whose administrative and strategical abilities and energies were devoted to bringing the war in Southeast Asia to the earliest possible conclusion.

An admiral who never exercised senior command at sea in combat (though he became First Sea Lord and Chairman of the Chiefs of Staff after the war), Mountbatten nonetheless served his nation in an important and demanding command position. At first distrusted by the Americans as a handsome "Royal Playboy," he soon showed them the daring, energy, and courage which had won him spectacular advancement in the Royal Navy.

There were many superb British seamen whose combat leadership undoubtedly warrants our consideration. Foremost among these, perhaps, would be Admiral Sir **Philip Vian,** who earned exceptional distinction as a destroyer commander, as a flotilla commander in at the kill of the *Bismarck*, and a fighting cruiser division commander under Cunningham in the Mediterranean. But to dwell upon men such as Vian would be unfair to the many others who fully maintained the traditions of the Royal Navy during World War II.

Royal Air Force Combat Commanders

"NEVER IN THE FIELD of human conflict was so much owed by so many to so few."

Such was the tribute of Winston Churchill to Fighter Command of the Royal Air Force after its great victory in the Battle of Britain.

At least four World War II battles have been suggested for inclusion among "The Decisive Battles of the World." But if Montgomery had lost at El Alamein, Rommel still would not have been able to reach the Suez Canal. And even if the Germans had won at Stalingrad a few months later, it was already too late for them to knock Russia out of the war; the best they could have achieved was a stalemate in the East. And had Yamamoto won at Midway, American determination and American resources still would have triumphed over Japan — even though the war would have lasted much longer and the cost would have been much greater.

But if Goering had won the Battle of Britain, World War II would have ended in 1940.

This was the one battle of the war which surely altered the trend of events, and decisively shaped the course of history. The man most responsible was Air Chief Marshal Sir **Hugh C. T. Dowding.** He started his military career in the army, but joined the Royal Flying Corps soon after its establishment in 1912, and served with great distinction throughout World War I. At the end of the war he was a squadron commander, and had been decorated several times.

In 1936 Dowding was appointed Commander in Chief of Fighter Command, entrusted with the air defense of Great Britain. He was responsible for the development, adoption, and perfection of a new and complicated system for ground control of defensive fighter

73

Marshal of the RAF Sir Hugh C. T. Dowding.

planes; the system was in full operation at the outset of the war. He was the man who accepted radar as the key element in this system, and who pressed for the installation of the great radar net which was built along the coasts of Britain just before war broke out. He was the man who selected the Hurricane and Spitfire fighter planes as the backbone of his command, and who established the requirements which resulted in the tremendous industrial effort which produced these planes in 1939 and 1940.

In May, 1940, Dowding estimated that with 50 squadrons — about 1,000 first-line fighter planes — he could surely defend Britain against full-scale German air assault. At that time he had a little more than three-fourths of this strength, but still felt the chances of a successful defense were reasonably good.

Then came the collapse of the French army and the French air force. The British Expeditionary Force needed air cover; and

Churchill also hoped that with British air support the French might still be able to continue the fight. At a Cabinet meeting Dowding said that with a minimum of 25 squadrons, or about 500 planes, he could still defend Britain, though the risk would be great; with less than that, success was unlikely. Churchill left him with this minimum force, and sent every additional fighter plane to France. After the French surrender, the remnants of the gallant British squadrons in France returned to England, giving Dowding only 550 operational planes. The margin was thin indeed!

The stirring and inspiring story of the Battle of Britain has been told elsewhere. The Germans were several times on the verge of success, but Dowding's slender margin was just enough, thanks to his skill and to the truly magnificent performance of his fighter pilots and their planes.

Churchill, in describing Dowding's dispositions in the crucial engagement of August 15, summed up the professional skill of this dour, quiet airman in the following words:

> The foresight of Air Marshal Dowding in his direction of Fighter Command deserves high praise, but even more remarkable had been the restraint and the exact measurement of formidable stresses which had reserved a fighter force in the North through all these long weeks of mortal conflict in the South. We must regard the generalship shown as an example of genius in the art of war.

By his victory in the Battle of Britain, Dowding warrants inclusion with the topmost ranks of British leaders, worthy of comparison with a soldier like Edward I* and a sailor like Nelson.

---

* Considered by this writer to be the greatest general in British history.

*Marshal of the RAF
Arthur T. Harris.*
Office of Chief of Naval
Operations

In February, 1942, Air Marshal **Arthur T. Harris** was appointed Commander in Chief of the RAF's Bomber Command. If Dowding had the honor of inflicting the war's most decisive defeat on Germany, Harris can probably claim credit for having punished Germany more severely than any other man during the war.

As a very young officer, Harris joined the Royal Flying Corps during World War I. Although his early service was in fighter planes, in the years just before World War II he and other far-sighted bomber enthusiasts of the Royal Air Force pioneered in the development of the concept of strategic air power — and of a doctrine for employing it.

Immediately after the Battle of Britain, Harris, then Deputy Chief of the Air Staff under Portal, was largely responsible for urging an immediate shift in British aircraft production from a concentration on fighter planes to building more bombers. Recognizing the decisive nature of Dowding's victory, Harris and Portal were determined that they would do everything they could to carry the war to Germany in a massive strategic air assault. Then, upon becoming Commander in Chief of Bomber Command, Harris was in a position to carry out his own concept. Immediately he bent every effort to the task, and did not relax for more than three years.

In May, 1942, barely three months after he had assumed his new command, Harris launched the first of many 1,000-plane raids against German industrial centers. This was an attack on Cologne, which was to suffer many more such raids before the war was over.

As American long-range bombing capabilities began to build up in Britain in 1943, Harris and Generals Spaatz and Eaker worked out an agreement to divide up the strategic bombing tasks. The more heavily armed and armored American bombers, with their improved bombsights, would strike point targets with precision bombardment in the daylight, while the heavily laden British Wellington and Lancaster bombers would blast regional targets at night in tremendously destructive mass raids.

During the war, and since, "Bomber" Harris has been accused by critics in his own country and elsewhere as having disregarded the laws of war by indiscriminate bombardment of the German civilian population. He has been accused of using terror tactics against the German people, rather than concentrating on truly military targets.

Such accusations bothered Harris not in the slightest. He never forgot the earlier indiscriminate German bombing raids against the cities of England, such as London and Coventry. But most important, he believed that his bombers were the only weapons that could bring military power to bear directly upon the war industry of Germany — and this, he believed, was a legitimate military target. These war industries, of course, were almost always located in or near great centers of population, and it was the civilians in these cities who were supporting the German war effort by working in the war industries. His planes concentrated their blows against the areas where key industries were located, but Harris saw nothing wrong in bringing the war directly to the people who were making it possible for Germany to make war. Though they were not in uniform, he considered that they were just as dangerous to his nation as were German soldiers or airmen.

The moral issue of strategic bombardment of cities — whether done by Germans, British, or Americans — is not one to be argued in this book. Right or wrong, Harris had the mission of carrying the war to Germany with his bombers, and he did the very best job that he could. By the time he was through, the Germans had paid manyfold for the damage they had inflicted on Britain.

Outstanding among the brilliant officers which the RAF developed in the years between the World Wars was **Arthur William Tedder.** After service in the Royal Flying Corps in France in World War I, Tedder had broad experience in training, operational command, and research and development in the years between the wars. In 1940 he was appointed Deputy Air Commander in Chief in the Middle East, and was responsible for providing the air support for Wavell's brilliant offensive in the Western Desert.

The following year Tedder became the senior air officer in the Middle East Theater, and in cooperation with his principal subordinate, Air Vice Marshal Arthur Coningham, began to develop a

Marshal of the RAF Sir Arthur William Tedder.
U.S. Army Photograph

new and more flexible system of tactical air support for ground troops. This system was largely perfected the following year in close and enthusiastic cooperation between Tedder, Coningham, and General Montgomery.

Tedder's success in supporting ground operations in the Middle East Command led to his appointment as Commander in Chief of the Allied Mediterranean Air Command, under General Eisenhower, in February, 1943. He worked closely with General Alexander, the ground commander, for the remainder of the year, controlling all Allied air operations in the Tunisian, Sicilian, and Italian campaigns.

Again success in supporting ground forces led Tedder to a new position. In late December, 1943, he was appointed Deputy Supreme Allied Commander for the invasion of Europe, directly under General Eisenhower. He served in this position for the rest of the war. His professional skill enabled him to contribute significantly to the air operations in the Normandy invasion and in the

Air Marshal Sir Arthur Coningham.
British Official Photograph

following campaigns until the surrender of Germany. Perhaps even more important was his wisdom and deftness in coordinating the activities of different services and different nationalities as Eisenhower's senior and most trusted subordinate.

The man most responsible for development of the technical and tactical details of British and (later) American air support in World War II was Air Vice Marshal **Arthur Coningham.** Born in Australia, he was still in his teens when he joined the New Zealand army at the outbreak of World War I, and initially saw service in Egypt as an infantryman and a cavalryman. When severe illness forced him out of the army in 1916, he immediately joined the Royal Flying Corps, serving with great distinction throughout the remainder of the war.

At the outset of World War II Coningham commanded a bomber group based in England. In July, 1941, he was appointed to command the Western Desert Air Force, under Tedder, in the Middle East. For the next two years he gave splendid air support to the

80

Eighth Army, and during this time worked with Tedder and Montgomery in elaborating tactical air doctrine.

In the following years Coningham followed Tedder, first as commander of the Tactical Air Forces of the Mediterranean Command, then as commander of the RAF 2d Tactical Air Force, supporting British ground forces in the invasion of Normandy and the subsequent campaigns in France and Germany.

Coningham was probably Britain's greatest air tactician of World War II. Perhaps not so gifted as Chennault in the details of aerial combat, he unquestionably had a clearer concept of the relationship of air power to land operation than did the great American fighter general.

Among the exceptionally large number of capable RAF professionals, it is difficult to single out others who were more outstanding than their fellows. Among those who warrant special consideration, perhaps, was Air Marshal **Sholto Douglas,** who had the perennial misfortune of taking over commands — such as Fighter Command and Middle East Command — after the scene of action had shifted to other areas. Another was Air Chief Marshal Sir **Trafford L. Leigh-Mallory** who performed capably as commander of the Allied Expeditionary Forces for the invasion of Europe, and who soon after died tragically in an air crash on his way to take over the air command in Southeast Asia. Slightly younger than these, but undoubtedly the intellectual star of the RAF, was **John C. Slessor,** who had become noted for his writings on strategy even before the war, who served as the chief planner on the Air Staff in the critical years 1942–43, and who then took over Coastal Command where he contributed to final Allied victory in the Battle of the Atlantic. Later, in 1944, Slessor became Deputy Air Commander in Chief in the Mediterranean.

Leaders Among the Other Allies

RUSSIA

IT IS NOT EASY to evaluate military leadership in Russia during World War II. Rigid Soviet censorship during the war, and carefully prepared official histories afterward, have had the common object of telling the outside world only what the Communist rulers of Russia thought was useful for propaganda purposes. The histories also see to it that Russian citizens are exposed only to "the party line." The histories have been carefully changed numerous times since the war as Russian political and military leaders have risen and fallen in official party favor.

The best source of information on Russian performance during World War II comes from captured German records, or reports prepared by German officers. These, of course, are not completely objective. The Germans wished to show how well they fought, and how they were overcome only by superiority in Russian numbers, not by good leadership. Though this is in part true, we have perhaps been influenced by German official records, and the postwar memoirs of German generals, to discount the ability of Russian commanders more than we should.

The Russian generals of World War II have produced no candid memoirs telling of their relations with each other and with their national leaders, as have the generals in Germany and other Western nations. Such memoirs are usually the best sources for leadership evaluation.

In short, evaluation of Russian military leadership in World War II is more chancy and less easily substantiated than in any other country. Only one thing is clear from the outcome of the war: there was much good leadership in Russia.

*Field Marshal Georgi
K. Zhukov.*
U.S. Army Photograph

Unquestionably the best Russian field commander was **Georgi K. Zhukov.** He had fought with great distinction as an enlisted man in World War I, winning four medals for bravery. He rose rapidly in the Red Army during and after the civil war. In 1938–39 he commanded Russian forces in Mongolia, and inflicted a severe defeat on the Japanese at the prolonged Battle of Halkin Gol. Then, early in 1941, he became Chief of Staff of the Russian army while still a relatively junior general; it should be remembered, however, that as army Chief of Staff, Zhukov was subordinate to Marshal Shaposhnikov, Chief of the General Staff.

During the dark days of the summer of 1941, when the Germans were crushing the Russian frontier armies, Zhukov went to the front — while still Chief of Staff — and personally took command of the defense of Smolensk, where he slowed down the German advance. Farther north, however, Marshal Voroshilov's army group, in front of Leningrad, was disintegrating. Stalin ordered Zhukov to Leningrad, where he took command on September 11, as German artillery was actually bombarding the city. In an amazing display of organizing genius and tactical skill, Zhukov completely reorganized the defending forces while repulsing the surprised Germans, who had expected to take the city easily. When he left a month later, the situation was stabilized, and the defense secure, though Leningrad was practically besieged.

The reason for his departure was another peremptory command from Stalin. The Germans had smashed their way to within striking distance of Moscow, and the Russian defenses there were crumbling. Stalin dismissed Marshal Timoshenko from command of the central front and put Zhukov in his place. The combination of Zhukov's skill, the arrival of reinforcements from Siberia, the exhaustion of the Germans, and the effect of bitterly cold weather upon the unprepared invaders, finally brought Hitler's advance to a halt in early December. But German tanks were actually in the suburbs of Moscow, and the city was almost encircled. Zhukov immediately counterattacked. More than anything else, perhaps, the vigor, perceptiveness, and powerful will shown by this decision are the hallmarks of great military leadership.

During the remainder of the war Zhukov became Stalin's principal handyman. The cautious and jealous dictator never placed him in overall command of the Red Army, or even of anything more than two or three army groups — and by the end of the war there were usually ten to twelve such groups operating along the entire front — but Zhukov was always sent to take command where the danger was greatest, or where success was most needed. He was the man who was entrusted with the defense of the Stalingrad region, and in the Russian counterattack he briefly commanded four army groups. He was then sent back to Leningrad, where he organized and began the great counteroffensive in the northern regions. Finally, he commanded the two principal army groups in the offensive against Berlin, and was primarily responsible for the capture of the German capital.

Many Red Army generals proved their fighting ability during the war. Zhukov was the only one who had an opportunity — and probably the only one with the ability — to be ranked with the very best leaders of the Germans, Americans, and British.

Marshal **Ivan S. Konev** was in some respects Zhukov's greatest rival as the leading Russian general during the war. While there is little doubt that Zhukov was the greater man, Konev was unquestionably a very able general. And though Konev was frequently under Zhukov's command — he was his deputy in the defense of Moscow — he seems to have become a rival in fact by the end of the war. He was also frequently entrusted by Stalin with the coordination of two or more army groups in important operations. He commanded two such groups in the final assault on Berlin, and seems to have been miffed by the credit which Zhukov received at the time. To this rivalry may in part be attributed the apparent sincerity of the article which Konev wrote in *Pravda* in 1957, after Zhukov's last fall from political favor, in which he belittled what Zhukov had done during the war.

Of the three topmost leaders at the outset of the war, Marshal **Semën K. Timoshenko** was a reasonably capable, plodding, unimaginative soldier; Marshal **Kliment E. Voroshilov** was more of a hack politician than a military man; Marshal **Semën M. Budënny** was a rather incompetent cavalry general who apparently was unable to adjust himself to the realities of modern war. All three owed their high rank to their party loyalty and to revolutionary ardor in the Russian civil war.

Several other Russian generals are worthy of mention. Among these are **Vasili I. Chuikov**, the tactical commander in Stalingrad who bore the brunt of that great battle; **Vasili D. Sokolovski,** who proved himself a very fine staff officer and commander under the guidance and influence of Zhukov; and **Konstantin K. Rokossovski** and **A. M. Vasilevski,** two other very capable protégés of Zhukov. Much credit for the unquestioned achievements of the Russian artillery was due to General **N. Voronov**, Chief of Artillery.

FRANCE

Little that is praiseworthy can be said of the original top war leadership of France. General **Maurice G. Gamelin** proved that he was not very good in fighting a World War I type of war, and totally incapable of coping with the German invasion. His successor, General **Maxime Weygand,** was unquestionably a more able man, who demonstrated vigor and determination, but by the time he came to command, the war was irretrievably lost, and he advocated surrender rather than continuing the war from Africa.

The most revealing measure of the French generals of 1940 is a comparison with their predecessors of 1914, under remarkably similar circumstances of unexpected and disastrous defeat. In 1914

*Marshal Jean de Lattre
de Tassigny.*
U.S. Army Photograph

French generals, no matter what the situation, tried to counter-attack whenever possible. In 1940 only one man attempted to counterattack; this was an obscure, relatively young tank commander, Brigadier General **Charles de Gaulle.** De Gaulle's principal role in World War II, however, was as a political and strategic leader, and will be given further attention in the next volume.

Jean de Lattre de Tassigny was wounded four times as a junior officer during World War I, and was seriously wounded in the Rif War in 1925. He was one of the few French division commanders who fought well during the Battle of France in 1940. Three times he repulsed German assaults across the Aisne River, and then, after withdrawal, tenaciously held the crossings of the Loire.

After the French surrender he served under the Vichy Government in Tunisia and in France. When the Germans overran southern France in November, 1942, he attempted to fight, but Premier

Laval had him arrested and thrown into prison, deprived of rank and honors. In September, 1943, he escaped and reached England, and then went to Algiers to offer his services to de Gaulle.

Early in 1944 de Lattre was placed in command of the French expeditionary force in Italy, replacing General Juin. In June he led a task force which captured the island of Elba. Then, in August, his Army "B" — soon to become the First French Army — followed the American VI Corps ashore in southern France. In company with the Americans, he pursued the Germans up the Rhone Valley and linked up with Eisenhower's armies, which were then sweeping eastward toward Germany. For the remainder of the war de Lattre and his French First Army were a part of Dever's 6th Army Group. Proud de Lattre was quick to take offense at any suggestion that France was a minor Allied partner. Nonetheless, he proved himself a brave, competent, and gallant ally. Though he did not have a chance to exercise independent high command during the war, de Lattre de Tassigny gave evidence of possessing true military genius, the greatest French soldier since Foch.

True military genius was also demonstrated by another French soldier, Philippe de Hautecloque, better known to history by the name he adopted during the war, **Jean Leclerc.** A young cavalry officer who had served with distinction in colonial combats, Captain de Hautecloque was captured by the Germans in May, 1940, in the Battle of Flanders. He escaped and rejoined the French army for the Battle of France, was wounded, recaptured, and escaped again, into Spain. Joining de Gaulle in London, he took the name Leclerc to avoid possible reprisals against his wife and children in France.

De Gaulle promoted Leclerc to major, and sent him to organize

General Jean Leclerc.
U.S. Army Photograph

Free French military forces in the Cameroons, in West Africa. Combining bravado with great courage and organizing ability, in a few months he had brought much of French Equatorial Africa under firm Free French control, and had established himself with a substantial military force near Lake Chad, close to the frontier of Italian Libya. During 1941 and 1942 he raided frequently across the Sahara against Italian oasis posts near the frontier.

Then, in December, 1942, Leclerc led a column of less than 3,300 men into southern Libya, which he conquered from the Italians. He then marched north to join Montgomery's Eighth Army at Tripoli in January, 1943. This tough desert column became the core of the French 2d Armored Division, which was recruited to full strength and provided with American equipment in Morocco, then sent to England to join the Allied invasion army. Arriving in Normandy in August, just after the breakout of Allied forces from the beachhead, Leclerc's division was rushed to Paris, where the Resistance was rising against the German garrison. Leclerc's division and the Resistance army liberated Paris in a bitter struggle, Leclerc receiving the German surrender on August 25.

For the remainder of the war Leclerc continued to command his 2d Armored Division with great distinction, but always under American command; he refused to serve under de Lattre due to an old and bitter personal enmity. It was a tragedy for France that this brilliant officer was killed in an airplane crash in Africa in November, 1947.

Alphonse Juin commanded a motorized division in the French First Army in northwestern France in May, 1940. His division was trapped by the German penetration through the Ardennes. Failing in an effort to break through the German tank columns, Juin and his division fought until their ammunition was exhausted, then surrendered in early June.

After a year as a prisoner of war, Juin was liberated at the request of General Weygand and sent to command Vichy forces in Morocco. He later commanded all French forces in North Africa. He fought reluctantly but stoutly against the Anglo-American invasion of November, 1942, surrendering on the orders of Admiral Darlan. He then willingly placed his army under the Allies, and turned it against the Germans in Tunisia.

In 1943 de Gaulle appointed Juin to command the French expeditionary force which participated in the invasion of Italy. Juin held this post until 1944, when de Gaulle appointed him as Chief of Staff of National Defense.

Marshal Alphonse Juin.
U.S. Army Photograph

Juin lacked the brilliance and flair of de Lattre and Leclerc; he was, however, a tough, competent professional who helped to restore honor and dignity to France by successful leadership of a revitalized, fighting French army.

CHINA

Overall standards of military leadership were lower in China than in any other major nation participating in World War II. There are a number of reasons for this, of which the most important was the fact that in the late nineteenth and early twentieth centuries military professionalism had declined greatly in China.

91

This was shown by the consistent inability of Chinese leaders and Chinese armies to stand up to the modern military forces of Japan or any Western nation. Training and schooling of officers was inadequate and often nonexistent. Chinese armies were not prepared to make efficient use of modern weapons of war, and their leaders were unable to cope with the problems of controlling, or of opposing, such weapons.

In the harsh training of warfare, however, some Chinese leaders rose above the generally low standards of their fellows. And military training and efficiency greatly improved under the overall guidance of Generalissimo Chiang Kai-shek, particularly after he became president of China in the late 1920's. Chiang, who had had an opportunity to receive military instruction in Japan, established a fairly good military school in China. Some of the best Nationalist and Communist Chinese leaders in World War II were graduates of Chiang's Whampoa Military Academy.

Probably the best of China's field commanders was General **Li Tsung-jên.** His greatest claim to military fame was as the commander of the group of Chinese armies which first defeated the Japanese in World War II, at Taierhchwang, in April, 1938. His principal assistant in that battle was General **Chang Tzu-chung,** who was later killed in action.

Next to the victory at Taierhchwang, the Chinese were proudest of the defense of Hengyang, in 1944, by a starving, bedraggled, exhausted army, which for forty-seven days repulsed determined attacks by larger and far more efficient Japanese forces. The commander of this gallant, and finally unsuccessful, effort was General **Fang Hsien-chueh,** who was able to make the most of his countrymen's unexcelled stubbornness in defense. Perhaps worthy of equal mention is General **Hsueh Yueh,** who won three small, but none-

General Li Tsung-jên with his wife, after he became president of Nationalist China.
U.S. Army Photograph

theless memorable, victories over Japanese forces at Changsha.

Among the other Chinese Nationalist generals who served Chiang against the Japanese were loyal and able General **Ho Ying-chin** — Chiang's chief of staff — **Yu Han-mou, Fu Tso-yi,** and the ordnance chief, **Yu Ta-Wei.** Mao Tse-tung's principal Communist military subordinates were Generals **Chu Teh** and **Lin Piao** — a graduate of Whampoa — both competent soldiers. Well known to Americans was General **Wei Li-huang,** who rather ineptly commanded Chinese forces in southwest China operating near the Burma-China frontier. Even better known to Americans were three very able division commanders who fought under Stilwell in Burma: American-educated **Sun Li-jen, Liao Yueh-shang,** and **Pan yu-kun.** None of these exercised high command during the war.

Among the lesser Allies a number of leaders became noted for failure as well as for success. We can mention only a few here.

Poland's Marshal **Edward Smigly-Rydz,** commander of the Polish army at the outset of the war, had an impossible task; he seems to have hastened his inevitable defeat by poor plans and inept leadership. After the collapse of the Polish armies, however, General **Wladyslaw Anders** commanded the Polish army in exile; he and his men distinguished themselves by their courage and fighting qualities in France, North Africa, and Italy.

General Wladyslaw Anders.
U.S. Army Photograph

General Alexander Papagos (right) with Admirals Nimitz and King. Office of War Information

Perhaps the most illustrious military leader of the smaller Allied nations was General **Alexander Papagos** of Greece. He inflicted stinging defeats on the Italian army that invaded his country in late 1940, and actually conquered the southern third of Italian Albania before Germany intervened in the Balkans. His exhausted, over-extended, and outnumbered troops were no match for the Germans, however, and Papagos was forced to surrender. But not before he had gallantly fought on without hope for several days, merely to give his English allies time to evacuate Greece.

Hopeless missions were also entrusted to two tough Dutch seamen in the Netherlands East Indies, when Japan began her whirlwind offensives into the islands and peninsulas of Southeast Asia. Vice Admiral **Conrad Helfrich** commanded Allied naval forces in Indonesian waters in February and March, 1942, and employed his scanty forces as capably as was possible under the circumstances. Brave Rear Admiral **Karel Doorman** led Allied forces in the disastrous Battle of the Java Sea, and sank with his flagship in a vain attempt to halt the superior Japanese invasion fleet.

Commanders in the Axis Forces

ONE OF THE MOST amazing military feats in history was the manner in which the German armed forces for three years fought the combined strength of America, Russia, and Britain, while at the same time keeping control over the seething Resistance movements of the rebellious peoples of conquered Europe. No matter what we may think of the German people for tolerating the leadership of a man like Hitler, we are forced to admire their determination and their fighting ability.

There are many reasons for this German fighting ability, which can be partly explained by psychologists, political scientists, sociologists, and anthropologists. Militarily, however, the exceptional fighting ability of the Germans, proven several times during the century before World War II, was due to their realization that modern war had been greatly complicated by scientific and technological developments of the Industrial Revolution. So the Germans, led by Prussia, created a General Staff to organize, plan, and control the waging of modern warfare. For political reasons which were peculiar to Germany, this General Staff also became a great political influence in the German Empire, and became a tool for conquerors like Kaiser Wilhelm and Hitler. But at the same time, the General Staff was able to develop the most efficient military organization in Europe. The German example was copied by all of the other great powers, but not until the time of World War II were any of the other countries in the world — most notably the United States — able to develop staffs of comparable military efficiency. We shall see in the next volume how Hitler ruined his nation's General Staff in World War II.

There are differences of opinions among military experts of Germany and of other nations as to which of Germany's many excellent generals were the best. The views of this writer may not be shared by many expert military specialists.

It is perhaps not fair to the surprisingly large number of competent German field commanders to devote serious attention to only a few. By briefly mentioning some of the many who contributed to the efficiency of the German war machine, however, it will be possible to indicate how uniformly high were the professional standards among its senior officers.

At the outset of the war, four senior generals exercised the very highest posts of command. Commander in Chief of the Army was General — later Field Marshal — **Walther von Brauchitsch.** A competent, energetic soldier, he never enjoyed the confidence of Hitler, and was not forceful enough to overcome the limitations placed upon him by the dictator. He was relieved from his command after the failure of the German attacks on Moscow, in December, 1941, when Hitler assumed personal command of the German army. He did not serve again.

Karl Rudolf Gerd von Rundstedt came from a noble Prussian family. Retired from active duty in late 1938, he was recalled in 1939 to command the Southern Army Group in the campaign against Poland. The following year his Army Group A played the principal role in the invasion of the West. For the invasion of Russia he commanded the Southern Army Group, which made the deepest and most spectacular advances into Russia.

In November, 1941, finding himself in complete disagreement with Hitler on the plans for a winter campaign, and with his recommendations ignored, Rundstedt resigned his command. In July,

1942, however, Hitler recalled him as Commander in Chief West, responsible for all German forces in France and the Low Countries. He retained his post until early July, 1944, shortly after the Allied breakout from the Normandy beachhead. It is reported that Hitler telephoned Rundstedt at his headquarters in Paris, asking advice. Rundstedt is supposed to have replied: "Make peace, you fool!" He was immediately relieved of his command, and replaced by von Kluge, who in turn was soon replaced by Model.

Yet, strangely, Hitler recalled Rundstedt to the same command a few months later, in September, after Model had stabilized the front in the West. Apparently Hitler felt that Rundstedt's presence would be reassuring to the tradition-minded officers of the army.

Rundstedt had, in fact, really ended his active military career when he gave up his command in Russia. He was merely a figurehead in both of his two periods of command in the West. This was partly due to the fact that Hitler never gave him the full authority that went with his title of Commander in Chief, and partly because the old soldier had lost the vigor and mental flexibility he had displayed in Poland and France. Beloved, respected, and trusted by his officers, Rundstedt was a model of the traditional Prussian officer. And though he made clear that he detested Hitler, he was also a model to most German officers in tolerating the continued tyranny of the Nazi dictator, and in allowing Hitler to ruin completely the country which they loved.

Fedor von Bock commanded the Northern Group of Armies in the invasion of Poland and the West, and he had the Center Group of Armies in the invasion of Russia. Relieved from his command because of ill health at the time his army group was halted at Moscow in December, 1941, Bock was brought back to command the Southern Army Group the following spring, but was again relieved in August when Hitler was infuriated by his failure to take Stalingrad. He did not serve actively again. Bock was a tough, fighting, aristocratic professional of the Rundstedt stamp.

Wilhelm von Leeb was another officer of that same traditional, professional, aristocratic stamp. He commanded the Southern Group of Armies in the invasion of France, and the Northern Group in the invasion of Russia. Like so many of Germany's fine generals, he was relieved by Hitler in December, 1941, when the Germans were halted by the Russians.

Outstanding among the younger leaders was **Erich von Man-**

stein, who was born Erich von Lewinski, son of a distinguished army officer, but was later adopted by his mother's brother-in-law, General von Manstein, an equally distinguished soldier. As a junior officer in World War I young Manstein served with distinction on the Western, Eastern, and Serbian fronts, and was badly wounded. Between the wars his brilliance caused him to be promoted to major general, and deputy to the Chief of the German General Staff.

Although he was in disfavor with Hitler at the outbreak of World War II, Manstein became chief of staff to von Rundstedt, who commanded the Southern Army Group in the Battle of Poland. He was still Rundstedt's chief of staff in 1939–40, when the latter was appointed to command Army Group A for the invasion of Western Europe.

It was at this time that Manstein's strategic brilliance first had a major influence on the war. He was very dissatisfied with the original plan of Hitler and von Brauchitsch, which he felt was a mere imitation of the Schlieffen Plan, by which Germany had almost won World War I. He believed that the Allies would be ready for such a plan, which could thus achieve only a partial victory in Holland and Belgium. With the strong support of von Rundstedt, he proposed instead a powerful surprise thrust through the Ardennes and northern France to the English Channel, thus isolating and destroying the left-flank Allied armies, and making it easy to overwhelm France with one more blow. Hitler, having heard rumors of a strategic controversy, sent for Manstein, and after hearing his opinion, revised the plan, which soon afterward worked out exactly as Manstein had envisaged.

Manstein commanded an infantry corps in the operations in Western Europe, and led an armored corps in the initial invasion of Russia. His brilliance led to his promotion to command of the

Eleventh Army, with which he conquered the Crimea and (in July, 1942) Sevastopol. His outstanding success in these operations (while the rest of the German army had been thrown back from Moscow and Leningrad) led to his promotion to Field Marshal. After briefly commanding the Northern Army Group, near Leningrad, late in 1942 Manstein was rushed to take command of the newly created Don Army Group, for the purpose of attempting the relief of the German forces cut off in Stalingrad. His slashing counterattacks would have been successful if Hitler had allowed General von Paulus to fight his way out to meet Manstein. But Hitler insisted that all ground be held, and thus doomed von Paulus' Sixth Army to destruction.

Not only did Manstein completely stop the Russian counteroffensive from Stalingrad, but in March, 1943, despite great Russian numerical superiority, he counterattacked in turn to win a victory in the Battle of Kharkov. This was the last important German victory of World War II.

During the remainder of 1943 and early 1944, Manstein commanded the Southern Army Group against the principal Russian offensives in the Ukraine. Although the Russian forces outnumbered his own by four- or five-to-one during this period, Manstein's brilliant withdrawals and counterattacks miraculously prevented a Russian breakthrough, and resulted in far heavier Russian casualties than those his own forces suffered. Hitler, however, refused to adopt his repeated recommendations for a further withdrawal, to shorter and more easily defended lines, where Manstein envisaged a showdown battle to knock Russia out of the war, or at least to gain a stalemate in the East. Hitler was infuriated by Manstein's obvious contempt for his military blunders, and in March, 1944, relieved him from command. Manstein took no further part in the war.

Manstein never exercised strategic command over an independent theater of operations, although he commanded about one quarter of the vast Russian front. For four and a half years, however, he demonstrated strategic, tactical, and administrative capabilities of the highest order, and seems to have had an inherent military genius unexcelled in Germany, and comparable to that of MacArthur.

Erwin Rommel is better known to the Western Allies than any of his countrymen primarily because of the brilliance of his operations against the British in North Africa. A bold, daring, chivalrous soldier, he won the respect — and even the reluctant admiration — of his British foes.

As a junior infantry officer in World War I, Rommel won his country's highest award for valor. He came to Hitler's attention as the commander of the dictator's personal headquarters in 1939. Promoted to command an armored division, Rommel led the invasion drive through the Ardennes and into northern France; his division was the first German unit to reach the English Channel.

As a corps commander, Rommel was sent by Hitler to North Africa early in 1941 in order to save Libya after Wavell's great victories over the Italians in the Western Desert. For most of the next two years Rommel and his Afrika Korps dominated the war in Libya and Egypt. Operating at the end of a long, insecure supply line, and never given sufficient support in terms of air power, reinforcements, or supplies, Rommel nevertheless won victory after victory. He took great risks, usually successfully. On those few occasions where luck deserted him, his skill quickly retrieved defeat and prevented disaster.

Field Marshal Erwin Rommel.
U.S. Army Photograph

Field Marshal Erich von Manstein
U.S. Army Photograph

Finally, however, the odds against him became too great, and he was overwhelmed by the forces of Alexander and Montgomery at the Battle of El Alamein in October, 1942. Despite radio orders from Hitler not to abandon his position, Rommel withdrew just in time to prevent the loss of his entire army, though he had to abandon most of his heavy equipment. He retreated across Libya to Tunisia, where he finally halted the closely pursuing forces of Montgomery.

Taking command of operations in Tunisia, early in 1943, Rommel then inflicted a sharp defeat on the American contingent of the Allied army at Kasserine Pass, but illness soon forced him to return to Germany. Allied victory in Tunisia was inevitable, due to superior strength, but it is hard to say how much longer the struggle might have been protracted had Rommel been able to remain in command.

After recovering, Rommel, now a field marshal, was placed in command of Army Group B defending the shores of Holland, Belgium, and France against expected Allied invasion. There he was under von Rundstedt, who commanded all German forces in the West.

Although Rommel had proven himself a master of mobile warfare, and believed in the utmost flexibility of operations by using mobile reserves, he came to the conclusion that this would not be possible along the invasion coast because of Allied air superiority. He was convinced that Allied control of the air would make it impossible to move large reserve forces quickly. For this reason, he felt that all of his troops should be deployed as close to the coast as possible, particularly in the areas where Allied landings were most likely: Normandy and the Dover Straits region. He believed that the only chance of success against an Allied invasion was to have strong forces close to the beach which could drive the Allies back into the water without having to wait for reinforcements that might never arrive.

Rundstedt disagreed with this concept. A strong believer in traditional German use of mobile reserves, he condemned Rommel's idea of a concentration close to the beaches as a "cordon defense," which would become useless if the Allies were able to break through at any place. Like most other senior German officers, he did not believe that Allied air power could be as effective as Rommel insisted it would be.

To Rommel's embarrassment, Hitler intervened in the argument and forced Rundstedt to adopt Rommel's plan, though only in part. The course of the Allied invasion proved Rommel to be right, although there is doubt whether even complete adherence to his plan could have driven the Allies off the Normandy beach-head. In any event, he continued to serve loyally under Rundstedt, despite some disagreements, and despite Hitler's continued inter-ference. Rommel was badly wounded in an Allied air raid, and was sent back to Germany to recuperate.

Before this he had become involved in the army plot against Hitler, and had agreed to become head of state if Hitler was over-thrown or killed. The plot failed on July 20, when Hitler miracu-lously escaped assassination. Rommel's part in the plot was dis-covered, and he was forced to swallow poison on October 14, 1944. Hitler did not want the German public to know that his favorite general, and the one most popular with the public, had turned against him.

Rommel was not popular, however, with many of his fellow officers. After the war several tried to belittle his reputation as having been made in an out-of-the-way theater in which only small forces were involved. They also tried to show that he was wrong in his concept of a non-mobile defensive strategy in Nor-mandy. The record, however, shows that Rommel's strategic con-cept in the southeastern Mediterranean was as brilliant as was his tactical command of a corps and an army in the most mobile field operations of World War II. It also shows that his abandonment of the mobile concept, when commanding an army group in France, was not because of his lack of understanding of the im-portance of mobile reserves, but was because he realized that under the circumstances his reserves could not be sufficiently mobile. Though his concept was for a rigid defense, by adopting it he was showing more mental flexibility than those who could

Field Marshal Albert Kesselring.
U.S. Army Photograph

not understand why the desirable doctrine had to be abandoned. In this writer's opinion Rommel was one of Germany's two greatest leaders of World War II.

Albert Kesselring was an army officer during most of his military career. However, in 1933 he was transferred from the artillery to the new (and still secret) *Luftwaffe,* or air force. He commanded air fleets in the invasions of Poland, Western Europe, and in the Battle of Britain. He was the senior air commander in the invasion of Russia.

In 1942 Kesselring was appointed Commander in Chief South, and thus was overall commander of German and Italian forces in the Mediterranean and North Africa. He had several personality clashes with his senior combat subordinate, Rommel. His first real opportunity to demonstrate his genius as a commander of combined forces came at the time of the Allied invasion of Italy, in late

106

1943. In his defensive campaigns in Italy for nearly two years he achieved the maximum possible results against far more numerous Allied forces. Because of his success in Italy, Hitler placed Kesselring in overall command of the Western Front in March, 1945, hoping that he could perform similar miracles along the Rhine. By this time Kesselring could do nothing even to delay the inevitable result.

Walter Model liked to call himself "the Führer's fireman." He proved his capability to put out apparently unquenchable fires on many occasions. He first came to Hitler's attention as a brilliant staff officer just before the war. He showed his command ability by leading a panzer division in the invasion of Russia. By early 1942 he had been promoted to the command of an army, and continued to distinguish himself on attack and in the defense.

Model lacked Manstein's keen strategic genius, but was one of Germany's finest tacticians during the war. Even before Manstein was relieved, Hitler had begun to use Model to take command of difficult spots. Late in 1943 he was promoted to command Army Group North, and checked the Russian winter offensive toward the Baltic States. After the relief of Manstein, Zhukov took advantage of the situation to break through the front of Army Group South; Model was rushed to the front, and miraculously plugged the hole and stopped the Russian drive. When the Russians then broke through north of the Pripet Marshes and headed toward Warsaw, Model was again shifted, and again stopped the Russian advance.

Then, with the Western Front splitting apart, as the Americans and British smashed their way out of the Normandy beachhead, Hitler called on Model to take command in the West and to perform another miracle — which he did. With the German armies

Field Marshal Walter Model.

apparently completely smashed in France, Model nonetheless succeeded in establishing a new and firm defensive line in Belgium and eastern France. Later, with Rundstedt recalled to command in the West, Model, commanding Army Group B, continued his brilliant defensive tactics in the bitter winter months of battles in Belgium and the Rhineland.

Although Model was always loyal to Hitler, he was never a spineless "yes-man." He was one of the few soldiers who could give his frank opinions to the dictator. Hitler took this from middle-class Model, while he would never take it from equally outspoken aristocratic officers like Manstein and Rundstedt. When he thought Hitler would refuse to permit withdrawals, Model simply acted, and informed the High Command afterward. He maintained this independence of mind to the very end; when resistance was hopeless in the Ruhr pocket, despite Hitler's orders to continue to fight, he ordered his troops to surrender, and then committed suicide.

Germany's leading panzer commander was **Heinz Guderian,** an outspoken tank force soldier who did much to build up Germany's armored strength before the war, and who was in large part responsible for developing the armored role in *blitzkrieg* tactics. He performed well in the command of large armored units in the invasions of Poland, France, and Russia. In the latter invasion he bitterly protested Hitler's diversion of his tank units from the drive on Moscow to the Kiev encirclement. Formerly a favorite of Hitler, his outspoken expression of opinion at this time, followed by the later failure of his tanks to take Moscow, in December, led to his abrupt dismissal from command.

In March, 1943, however, Guderian was called back as Inspector General of panzer troops, and was appointed acting Chief of Staff of the army in July, 1944, following the unsuccessful assassination attempt on Hitler. He was relieved again, following an argument with Hitler, in March, 1945. Lacking the spark of exceptional genius of a Manstein or a Rommel, Guderian was, nonetheless, one of the finest fighting soldiers of the war; a worthy counterpart of America's Patton.

Paul L. E. von Kleist first commanded armored forces when, in the spring of 1940, his seniority led to his appointment in command of the panzer group, or armored army, which spearheaded the drive through the Ardennes and northern France. Despite a personality clash with Guderian, who commanded a corps in his army, Kleist performed well, and undoubtedly learned much about tank warfare from his temperamental subordinate. His tanks spearheaded the invasion of the Balkans in April, 1941, and in June of that same year he led another panzer group in the forefront of Rundstedt's army group into the Ukraine. His tanks led the great drive into the Caucasus in the summer of 1942. When that offensive failed, due to overextension and the repulse at Stalingrad, Kleist was given command of newly established Army Group A, and conducted a splendid withdrawal back to the Sea of Azov and the Crimea. For the following year and a half his small army group anchored the right flank of the German line in southern Russia. He was relieved from his command at the same time as Manstein. Lacking the flair of Guderian, he was an excellent armored force commander, and performed creditably as an army group commander.

The one German military man who came measurably close to winning the war with the forces under his command was Grand Admiral **Karl Doenitz**. He had been a submarine officer in World War I, and was placed in command of the new German U-boat force when it was created by Hitler's order in 1935. Doenitz carefully studied the records of World War I submarine operations, in which German U-boats had nearly starved Britain into surrender. On the basis of his studies he developed new submarine tactics and new technical improvements. He was a resolute and driving leader who insisted upon meticulous training and tight discipline. His subordinate officers and men probably never loved this tall, brooding, austere man, but they had unbounded admiration and respect for him. Thus, right up to the end of the war, and despite catastrophic losses at sea, he was able to maintain high morale and efficiency in Germany's underseas fleet.

Doenitz devised the highly effective "wolf-pack" tactics, which came very close to cutting Britain's supply lines. He kept tight personal control by radio over the operations of his submarines at sea, and was able to maneuver individual boats and wolf-pack groups so as to inflict the greatest possible damage upon the Allied sea-lanes. He was personally inventive and imaginative, and right

Grand Admiral Karl Doenitz in his cell, awaiting trial as a war criminal.
U.S. Army Photograph

to the end of the war kept developing new tactics, new techniques, new technical improvements, and even an entirely new kind of submarine, in a desperate effort to keep his submarines offensively and defensively ahead of Allied countermeasures. In the end he was unsuccessful, but it was a very close battle, and the Allied victory was primarily due to the tremendous shipbuilding capacity of the United States — to build more merchant ships than Doenitz' boats could sink, and an overwhelmingly superior force of small escort warships. Combined with this industrial power were the intensified efforts of the best scientific and naval brains in the United States and Britain.

At the very end of the war, after the suicide of Hitler, Doenitz became German chief of state, and negotiated the final surrender of the shattered German armed forces to the Allies.

After the war Doenitz was tried and convicted of being a war criminal at the famous Nuremberg trials of leading Nazis and

111

German military men. He was convicted and sentenced to ten years in prison primarily because he had ordered his submarines to stop rescuing Allied survivors of their submarine attacks. Since he had given this order only after Allied planes had attacked one of his submarines while it was trying to rescue survivors, many military men believe that Doenitz' conviction was not justified.

Doenitz had become the commander in chief of the entire German navy in 1943 after the resignation of Grand Admiral **Erich Raeder.** Raeder had been chief of staff to Admiral von Hipper — one of Germany's greatest naval heroes — in World War I. He became commander in chief of the navy in 1935, and had played a great role in the rapid buildup of German naval strength in the years just prior to the war. Raeder probably understood the relationship of sea power to land power better than anyone else in Germany, and tried to make Hitler aware of the importance of this relationship. He was unsuccessful; Hitler generally overruled his recommendations, and forced him to fritter away the German surface fleet in operations which Raeder opposed. Finally, his frustration at Hitler's orders led Raeder to resign, in January, 1943.

Like Doenitz, Raeder was tried by the Allied tribunal at Nuremberg after the war, and served ten years in prison. Many Allied military men also believe that this conviction was unfair.

JAPAN

With a few exceptions the Japanese top military leadership was inferior to the higher command echelons of the United States, Britain, and Germany. It is difficult to characterize exactly how and why most Japanese military commanders failed to measure up to their European and American counterparts, since they were, for the most part, well-trained, intelligent, and dedicated professionals, and the products of a long and proud military tradition. Yet they were, for the most part, rather unimaginative. They tended to react to situations in a rather rigid and predictable fashion, and were often confused by anything unexpected. Even their most brilliant performances — of which there were many — were often spoiled by inexplicable failures or lapses in planning or in execution.

On balance, the standards of leadership of the Japanese navy were slightly higher than those of the army. Japanese admirals seem to have had a bit more strategic vision than the average Japanese general. Technically and tactically, the Japanese navy was generally on a par with those of the United States and Britain, and in some significant aspects was superior to those navies. Great competence was shown in several victories which the Japanese navy won in 1941 and 1942. Yet there were many instances in those years in which Japanese naval forces failed to take advantage of success, or in which surprising blunders cost them the fruits of hard-won triumphs.

Japan's leading strategist, and the man who probably recognized most clearly the dangers of starting a war with the United States, was Admiral **Isoroku Yamamoto.** A veteran of the Russo-Japanese War and of World War I, Yamamoto had been responsible for the development of Japan's naval air arm in the 1920's and 1930's. In 1941 he became the chief of Japan's Combined Fleet. Although he opposed war with the United States, because of his awareness of the potential industrial power of America, he did all he could to make the Japanese navy ready. Recognizing that Japan's only hope for victory in a Pacific war would be to gain control of the Pacific at the outset, he devised the strategic plan for the attack on Pearl Harbor.

Shortly after the war began, Yamamoto was popularly misquoted in the United States as having boasted that he planned to "sign a peace treaty in the White House." In fact, Yamamoto, recognizing the inherent toughness of the American people, had merely warned his optimistic countrymen that they could not expect a victory over the Americans unless they were able to dictate peace terms in the White House.

Despite his doubts, Yamamoto did everything in his power to win. Yet his complicated plan for the advance against Midway, which resulted in serious dispersion of the Japanese fleet over the Central Pacific, helped the Americans win at Midway. The following year, while inspecting Japanese defenses in the northern Solomon Islands, Yamamoto's plane was shot down by American planes over Bougainville; he and several members of his staff were killed. His death deprived Japan of her most gifted strategist and most effective fleet commander.

The man directly responsible for Japan's most spectacular naval victories was Admiral **Chuichi Nagumo,** who commanded the Japanese First Air Fleet at the outset of the war. Nagumo's carrier planes won the great Japanese victory at Pearl Harbor. He then went on to attack northwestern Australia, to assist in the conquest of the Netherlands East Indies, and, following that, to sweep the Indian Ocean as far as the coasts of Ceylon and India. After losing four carriers in the Battle of Midway, Nagumo seems also to have lost his nerve and his effectiveness. He was relieved of his command of the Japanese carrier force in 1943. He later was placed in command of a small naval flotilla in the Marianas, and was there at the time of the American invasion. About July 1, 1944, shortly before American forces conquered the island of Saipan, he committed suicide on the island. Nagumo was a competent, hard-fighting sailor; he was not a great naval commander.

Admiral Yamamoto's successor as Commander in Chief of the Combined Fleet was Admiral **Mineichi Koga.** He lacked both the aggressiveness and the skill of Yamamoto. In the Solomons and the Bismarcks he frittered away the air strength that Yamamoto had rebuilt in the carrier force of the fleet. Partly because of this loss of his striking force, and partly because of his unwillingness to risk major surface action, he kept his fleet almost continuously in the relative safety of the Truk anchorage. When the American Navy began to drive into the Marshall Islands, early in 1944, Truk was badly battered and Koga decided to withdraw his fleet to the Palaus and Singapore. Intensified American carrier air attacks against the Palaus in late March, 1944, caused Koga to decide to withdraw still farther, to the Philippines. During the withdrawal he died in a plane crash near Mindanao, on March 31 or April 1. In eleven months he had added neither glory nor strength to the Combined Fleet.

Much more aggressive than Koga was Admiral **Soemu Toyoda,** Koga's successor in command of the Combined Air Fleet. He immediately began to rebuild the depleted carrier air strength of the fleet, but had only partially accomplished this objective when the Americans began their invasion of the Marianas. Toyoda sent most of his fleet out to interfere with the invasions, but a combination of faulty tactics on the part of his principal subordinate, and the inexperience of the newly trained carrier pilots, led to disastrous Japanese losses in the Battle of the Philippine Sea.

Toyoda was again forced to rebuild his carrier striking forces

115

from scratch. At the same time he conceived the *"Sho"* (Victory) naval plan for defending the Philippines and Formosa against an expected American assault. When this came in October, 1944, Toyoda allowed himself to be tricked by Halsey into committing his new carrier squadrons piecemeal into the air battle off Formosa. The result was the destruction of the bulk of Japanese naval air fighting strength for the fourth time in the war.

Although Toyoda's surface and air strategy completely fooled Halsey in the subsequent Battle for Leyte Gulf, American naval strength was so overwhelmingly superior that the Japanese navy was destroyed as a major combat force. Like Yamamoto, Toyoda was a man of vigor and of determination. Like Yamamoto, also, he liked complicated operational plans that were difficult, if not impossible, to carry out in the heat of battle. He did not, however, have the clear, strategic vision of Yamamoto, though of course the opportunities available to him were far more limited.

Among other Japanese admirals of ability, **Abe, Kondo, Inouye, Ozawa, Nishimura, Shima,** and **Kurita** all deserve mention. All caused serious losses to the Americans, at one time or another, before they eventually suffered severe defeat at the hands of the United States Navy. Two junior admirals, however, caused the Americans more troubles and losses than these senior naval commanders. One of these was Rear Admiral **Gunichi Mikawa,** who inflicted the humiliating defeat of Savo Island on a larger Allied force off Guadalcanal. The other was Rear Admiral **Raizo Tanaka,** who repeatedly outwitted his American opponents in resupplying and reinforcing the land garrison of Guadalcanal during the prolonged struggle for that island, and who proved himself to be a brilliant destroyer tactician during these and subsequent naval engagements in the Solomons.

No single Japanese land commander had the same far-reaching strategic opportunities which were available at one time or another to Admirals Yamamoto, Koga, Toyoda, and Nagumo. Field Marshal Count **Juichi Terauchi** perhaps came the closest, since he exercised senior command in China in the early days of the war, and later held at least nominal command over Japanese land forces in Southeast Asia, the Philippines, and Indonesia. However, both the original Japanese offensive strategy, and the subsequent Allied counteroffensives were such that there was little coordination of operation in any of the different regions — and, in fact, such coordination was almost impossible for the Japanese in the late stages of the war. Thus Terauchi remained most of the time in Indochina, and had little to do with any of the widespread activities in his area of responsibility.

The Japanese ground commander who had the most opportunity to demonstrate his ability was General **Tomoyuki Yamashita.** His invasion of Malaya and subsequent conquest of Singapore comprised one of the very finest single campaigns of the Asiatic-Pacific war. Later he succeeded mediocre General **Masaharu Homma,** who had not particularly distinguished himself in the conquest of the Philippines. Yamashita greatly improved the readiness of Japanese forces there for the American invasion. He was ruthless in his efforts to suppress American and Philippine Resistance activities in the Philippines. When the American invasion came, he performed as well as could have been expected in the light of overwhelming American naval and air superiority.

After the war Yamashita was tried as a war criminal because of the cruelty with which some of his subordinates carried out his orders to put down the Resistance. Many American military men believe that the trial was not fair, that Yamashita was improperly

General Tomoyuki Yamashita on trial as a war criminal.
U.S. Army Photo

convicted, and that General MacArthur was too hasty in ordering his immediate execution without allowing him adequate opportunity for appeal. MacArthur, and most of the Filipino people as well, could not forget, however, the ruthlessness of Yamashita's military government in the Philippines, and the many bloody outrages which he condoned.

Another very able Japanese tactician was General **Shojiro Iido,** conqueror of Burma in 1942. The speed, vigor, and efficiency of his campaign were fully comparable to the qualities displayed by Yamashita in Malaya. After the conquest, however, Iido was superseded by more senior General **Shoze Kawabe,** who planned and directed the spectacular Japanese invasion of India in early 1944. When that invasion, after tremendous initial success, finally crumbled into costly disaster, Kawabe was relieved. His successor was General **Hoyotaro Kimura,** whose plans for the defense of Burma against superior Allied invasion forces were commendable. However, he allowed himself to be badly tricked by British General Slim, and was decisively defeated in the subsequent battles for control of Central Burma. In these battles, Lieutenant General **Shinichi Tanaka,** Kimura's deputy, greatly distinguished himself, and was largely responsible for the masterful withdrawal of the remnants of the Japanese force toward Thailand.

In the Pacific islands the local Japanese commanders had little opportunity to demonstrate anything save determination and tough fighting ability. For the most part they were outmaneuvered by the Americans and, as a result, Japanese losses were usually far greater than those of their opponents.

ITALY

The performance of Italian military forces in World War II was probably the poorest of any major participants in the war. There was little to choose between the army, the navy, and the air force. An Allied naval joke about the Italian navy was typical of what their opponents and allies thought of them. A comparison of the drinking interests of the sailors of three nations was supposed to go like this: American sailors like whiskey, English sailors prefer rum, but Italian sailors stick to port.

Italian forces collapsed in the face of determined Allied onslaughts in North Africa, in the Mediterranean, and later in Sicily. With German support, and under the leadership of Rommel, some Italian troops did fight valiantly for a while in North Africa. Similar German troop support and command under German General Hube prolonged Italian resistance in Sicily. But under their own inept commanders, Italian forces were uniformly unsuccessful.

The one senior Italian leader who emerged from the war without loss of honor was Marshal **Pietro Badoglio.** He had served with considerable distinction in World War I, and in the years between the wars. He commanded the Italian armies that conquered Abyssinia in 1935–36, and was appointed Governor General of Abyssinia. In June, 1940, he was appointed chief of staff of the Italian armies. He opposed Mussolini's decision to try to conquer Greece, and resigned in December, 1940, after the army of General **Visconti-Prasca** was ignominiously defeated by Greek General Papagos. In 1943 Badoglio was the leader of the widespread plot which overthrew Mussolini, and he was made premier. When the Germans took over most of Italy, Badoglio and most of his government fled to the south, where they joined the Allied armies. Badoglio continued to direct the subsequent successful Italian participation in the war against Germany until June, 1944, when he retired.

The grandest military name in Italy at the outset of World War II was that of Prince **Amedeo Umberto, Duke of Aosta.** Son of a noted Italian general of World War I, he was viceroy of Italian East Africa when the war began. When his forces overran British Somaliland (after the British withdrew), Mussolini expected Aosta to follow with the conquest of the Nile Valley and of Tanganyika. However, before that could happen, Italian East Africa was invaded by much smaller, but much more determined, British forces, and Aosta was soon forced to surrender ignominiously.

This performance was matched by that of equally vainglorious Marshal **Rodolfo Graziani,** who commanded Italian forces in Libya in 1940, when Italy declared war on Britain. Despite a tremendous numerical superiority, Graziani moved very cautiously a few miles across the border into Egypt, then stopped and fortified his encampments. Later in the year he was overwhelmed by Wavell's offensive and fled ignominiously back to Libya, where he resigned his command.

Again it must be noted that despite the very poor showing of Italian forces, and particularly of their commanders, in the early days of the war, the Italian army and its officers fought vigorously and honorably when they turned against the Germans and joined the Allies in an eventually successful effort to liberate their nation.

Index

Alexander, Field Marshall Sir Harold, R. L. G.: author's evaluation of, 58; in Burma, 57, 58; as Commander in Chief, Middle East Command, 58; as commander of ground forces, Sicily and Italy, 58; as Deputy Supreme Commander, Mediterranean Theater, 58; as division commander at Dunkirk, 56; as field force commander, Tunisia, 58; as Supreme Commander, Mediterranean Theater, 58; temperament of, 56

Anders, General Wladyslaw: author's evaluation of, 94; commands Polish armies in exile, 94

Auchinleck, General Claude J. E.: author's evaluation of, throughout; as Commander in Chief, India; as Commander in Chief, Middle East, 59; as commander, Narvik expedition, 59; defeat at El Gazala, 59; reorganizes Western Desert Force, 59; replaced by Alexander, 59; and Rommel, 59; in W.W. I, 59

Badoglio, Marshal Pietro: appointed Chief of Staff of Italian armies, 119; author's evaluation of, 119; and conquest of Abyssinia, 119; cooperation with Allies against Germany, 120; differences with Mussolini, 120; and plot to overthrow Mussolini, 120; as premier of Italy, 120

Bock, General Fedor von: author's evaluation of, 99; as commander of army groups in Poland, the West, and Russia, 99; relieved of command, 99

Bradley, General of the Army Omar N.: author's evaluation of, 7; as commander of American First Army in Normandy invasion, 7; as commander of American Twelfth Army Group, 7; as commander of First, Ninth, and Fifteenth Armies, 7; as "GI's General," 5; with Seventh Army, 6; in Tunisia, 6

Brauchitsch, Field Marshal Walther von: author's evaluation of, 97; as Commander in Chief of German army, 97; relations with Hitler, 97; relieved of command, 97

British Royal Air Force, author's evaluation of, 73

British Royal Navy in World War II, summary and author's evaluation of, 62, 63

Buckner, Simon Bolivar, Jr.: author's evaluation of, 25; death of, 25; at Okinawa, 24, 25

Budënny, Marshal Semën M.: author's evaluation of, 86

Chennault, Major General Claire L.: and Chiang Kai-shek, 41, 42; as aerial tactician, 41; author's evaluation of, 41, 42; establishes Flying Tigers, 42; and General Stilwell, 42; retirement, 41

Chinese generals: author's evaluation of, 92, 93; Chang Tsu-chung, 92; Chu Teh, 93; Fang Hsien-chue, 92; Fu Tso-yi, 93; Ho Ying-chin, 93; Hsueh Yueh, 92; Liao Yuh Shang, 93; Lin Pao, 93; Li Tsung-jen, 92; Pan Yu-kun, 93; Sun Li-jen, 93

Chinese military leadership, author's evaluation of, 91, 92

Clark, General Mark W.: author's evaluation of, 14; as commander of Allied Fifteenth Army Group, 13; as commander of Fifth Army in Italy, 13; and secret conferences in Algiers, 13

Coningham, Air Marshal Sir Arthur: author's evaluation of, 81; as commander of bombing group, 80; as commander of RAF 2nd Tactical Air Force, 81; as commander of Western Desert Air Force, 80, 81; in W.W. I, 80

Cunningham, Admiral of the Fleet Sir Andrew B.: and air raid on Italian fleet, 64; author's evaluation of, 65; as Commander of Mediterranean Fleet, 64; and control of Mediterranean, 65; as convoy commander, 64; and destruction of British fleet, 64; encounters with Italian fleet, 64; evacuates British troops from Crete and Greece, 64; as First Sea Lord, 65; and surrender of Italian fleet, 65

Devers, General Jacob L.: author's evaluation of, 8; in Alsace, Rhineland, and southwest Germany, 8; as commander of Armored Force, 7; as commander of Sixth Army Group, 7; as commanding General of European Theater of Operations, 7;

as Deputy Supreme Allied Commander, Mediterranean Theater; as division commander in buildup of American Army, 1940, 7; "forgotten general," 7

Doenitz, Grand Admiral Karl: author's evaluation of, throughout; as commander of German U-boat force, 110; conviction as war criminal, 112; develops tactical and technical improvements in submarine warfare, 110, 111; as German chief of state, 111; qualities as leader, 110

Doolittle, Lieutenant General James H.: author's evaluation of, 44; as commander of Eighth, Twelfth, and Fifteenth Air Forces, 42; develops "blind flying," 43; in air assaults against Japan, 44; as leader of raid on Japan, 43; record as private flyer, 43; record in Regular Army Air Corps, 42; resigns from Air Corps, 43

Doorman, Admiral Karel: author's evaluation of, 95; in Battle of Java Sea, 95; death of, 95

Douglas, Air Marshal Sholto: author's evaluation of, 81

Dowding, Air Marshal of the RAF Sir Hugh C.T.: author's evaluation of, 75; and Battle of Britain, 75; Churchill's tribute to, 75; as Commander in Chief, Fighter Command, 73, 74; in W.W. I, 73

Eaker, General Ira C.: as commander of Eighth Air Force, 47; as commander of Mediterranean Allied Air Forces, 47; as senior division commander, Eighth Air Force, 47; in bombing of Western Europe, 47

Eichelberger, General Robert L.: author's evaluation of, 24; as commander of Eighth Army, 23; put in charge of American-Australian force at Gona-Buna, 23; victory in the Pacific, 23

Eisenhower, General of the Army Dwight D.: author's evaluation of, 4, 5; as commander of U.S. forces in England and "Operation Torch," 2; criticism of, 3, 4; as general of the U.S. Army, 3; as military diplomat, 3; as Supreme Allied Commander for European invasion, 3

Fraser, Admiral Sir Bruce: author's evaluation of, 66; as commander of British Home Fleet, 66; as commander of British Pacific Fleet, 66; encounter with

Scharnhorst, 66; as Third Sea Lord, 66

French military leadership, author's evaluation of, 86, 87

Gamelin, Maurice G.: author's evaluation of, 86

German military leaders, author's evaluation of, 96, 97

Graziani, Marshal Rodolfo: as commander of Italian forces in Libya, 120; defeated by Wavell, 120

Guderian, General Heinz: author's evaluation of, 109; responsibility for role of armored units in *blitzkrieg,* 109; as commander of armored units in Poland, France, and Russia, 109; differences with Hitler, 109; dismissal from command, 109; recalled to duty as Inspector General of panzer troops, 109; relieved of command for second time, 109

Halsey, Fleet Admiral William F.: author's evaluation of, 32; at Leyte Gulf, 32; as naval professional, 31; in operational control of Central Pacific Naval Forces, 32; raids on Japanese coast and in South China Sea, 32; role in smashing Japanese air might, 32

Harris, Marshal of the RAF Sir Arthur T.: author's evaluation of, 78; and bombing of Germany, 77, 78; as Commander in Chief of Bomber Command, 77; as Deputy Chief of Air Staff, 76, 77; as pioneer in strategic air power; with Royal Flying Corps, 76

Helfrich, Vice Admiral Conrad: as commander of Allied naval forces in Indonesian waters, 95; author's evaluation of, 95

Hewitt, Admiral Henry K.: author's evaluation of, 37; as amphibious specialist, 37; as commander of naval support forces in Moroccan landings, 37; as leader of landing operations in Sicily, Salerno, and northern France, 37

Hodges, General Courtney H.: author's evaluation of, 11; and American First Army, 11

Homma, General Masaharu: author's evaluation of, 117; and conquest of the Philippines, 117; and invasion of the Philippines, 117; suppresses Resistance activities, 117

Iido, General Shojiro: author's evaluation of, 118; and conquest of Burma, 118; as military tactician, 118

Ingersoll, Admiral Royal E.: author's evaluation of, 36; as commander of Atlantic Fleet, 1942–1944, 36; conducting of all troop convoys to Europe, 36; responsibility for victory against German submarines in Atlantic, 36; as supervisor of major amphibious operations in Europe, 36

Ingram, Admiral Jonas H.: as commander of Atlantic Fleet, 36, 37; as successor to Ingersoll, 37

Italian military forces, author's evaluation of, 119, 120

Japanese admirals, mentioned: Abe, Inouye, Kondo, Kurita, Nishimura, Ozawa, Shima, 116

Japanese military leaders, author's evaluation of, 113

Juin, Marshal Alphonse: with Allied forces in Tunisia, 90; appointed Chief of National Defense, 90; author's evaluation of, 91; commands French forces in North Africa, 90; imprisonment and release, 90; surrenders to Allies, 90; surrenders to Germans, 91; with Vichy-French, 90

Kawabe, General Shoze: and Japanese invasion of India, 118

Kenney, General George C.: author's evaluation of, 48; as combat pilot, W.W. I, 48; as commander of Southwest Pacific Allied Air Forces, 48; develops operational tactical air support in the Pacific, 49; originates skip-bombing technique, 49

Kesselring, Field Marshal Albert: clashes with Rommel, 106; commands *Luftwaffe* in invasion of Poland, Western Europe, and Battle of Britain, 106; in defensive campaigns in Italy, 107; as overall commander of German and Italian forces in the Mediterranean and North Africa, 106; as overall commander on Western Front, 107

Kimura, General Hoyotaro: author's evaluation of, 118; defeat in Central Burma, 118; role in defense of Burma, 118

Kinkaid, Admiral Thomas C.: author's evaluation of, 32, 33; as commander of Seventh Fleet, 33; as commander of carrier task force in South Pacific, 33; as cruiser commander in Battles of Coral Sea and Midway, 32, 33

Kirk, Admiral Alan A.: author's evaluation of, 37; as commander of naval forces in Normandy invasion, 37

Kleist, General Paul L. E. von: author's evaluation of, 110; commands panzer group in France, 109; differences with Guderian, 109; relieved of command, 110; with Rundstedt in the Ukraine, 109; in second invasion of the Balkans, 109

Koga, Admiral Mineichi: author's evaluation of, 115; Commander in Chief of Japanese Combined Fleet, 115; compared with Yamamoto, 115; death of, 115; withdraws Japanese fleet to Philippines, 115

Konev, General Ivan S.: article on Zhukov, 85; author's evaluation of, 85; in Berlin assault; in defense of Moscow, 85

Krueger, General Walter: author's evaluation of, 23; as commander of Sixth Army, Southwest Pacific Command, 23; in New Guinea, New Britain, Leyte, and Luzon, 23; as tactician and disciplinarian, 23

Leclerc, General Jean: with Allied forces in Normandy invasion, 90; author's evaluation of, throughout; captured by Germans, 88; death of, 90; and de Gaulle, 88, 89; escape from Germans, 88; organizes Free French forces in West Africa, 88, 89; with Resistance army in liberation of France, 90; serves under American command, 90; in southern Italy, 89

Leeb, General Wilhelm von: as commander in invasions of France and Russia, 99; relieved of command, 99

Leigh-Mallory, Air Chief Marshal Sir Trafford L.: author's evaluation of, 81

LeMay, General Curtis E.: author's evaluation of, throughout; as commander of America's Strategic Air Command, 45; as commander of B-29 Superfortresses, 44; as commander of Fourteenth Air Force, 44; and development of bombardment tactics, 44; and incendiary raids on Japan, 44; as leader of XX and XXI Bomber Commands, 44

MacArthur, General of the Army Douglas: admirers and critics of, 16; and Allied drive from Australia to Japan, 17; as Army Chief of Staff, 16; author's evaluation of, 17, 18; as commander of Allied forces in Southwest Pacific, 17; as commander of Philippine Commonwealth's armed forces, 16; as commander of U.S. and Philippine armed forces in Far East, 16; in W.W. I, 16

Manstein, Field Marshal Erich von: author's evaluation of, throughout; as Chief of Staff to von Rundstedt, 100; as commander of German Eleventh Army Group, 101, 102; as commander of German Southern Army Group in Ukraine, 101; as deputy to German General Staff, 100; differences with Hitler, 100; and invasion of Russia, 100; relieved of command, 101; victory at Kharkhov, 101

Marines, U. S., the: reason for large number of casualties among, 38; role in the Pacific War, 37

Mikawa, Rear Admiral Gunichi: and defeat of Allies at Savo Island, 116

Military leadership in Russia, 82

Mitscher, Admiral Mark A.: author's evaluation of, 35; as commander of Task Force 58; defeat of Japanese in Solomon Islands, 35; role in prewar development of naval aviation, 35

Model, Field Marshal Walter: author's evaluation of, 108; checks Russian offensive, 107; as commander of German Army Group B, 108; Hitler's recognition of, 107; as military tactician, 107; promoted to army commander, 107; in Russian invasion, 107; stops Allied drive in Belgium and eastern France, 108; stops Russian advance on Warsaw, 107; suicide of, 108

Montgomery, Field Marshal Bernard L.: at Alam el Halfa, 55; author's evaluation of, 56; in Battle of El Alamein, 56; as commander of British Eighth Army, 55; as division leader in British Expeditionary Force in France, 54

Mountbatten, Admiral of the Fleet Lord Louis: author's evaluation of, 72; as commander of Combined Operations, 71; as destroyer commander, W.W. II, 71;

as Supreme Commander of Allied Southeast Asia Command, 71, 72; in W.W. I, 7

Nagumo, Admiral Chiuchi: author's evaluation of, 115; in attack on Pearl Harbor, 114; in attacks on Australia and Netherlands East Indies, 114; in command and flotilla in Marianas, 114; defeat at Midway, 114; in Indian Ocean, 114; responsibility for Japanese naval victories, 114; suicide of, 115

Nimitz, Fleet Admiral Chester W.: author's evaluation of, 29; in Battle of the Coral Sea, 28; as director of naval and amphibious operations in the Pacific Ocean areas, 27; at Japanese surrender, 28

Pacific naval commanders mentioned: Bartley, Admiral Daniel E., 36; Fletcher, Admiral Frank Jack, 36; Hart, Admiral Thomas C., 36; Wilkinson, Admiral Theodore S., 36; author's evaluation of, 36

Papagos, General Alexander: author's evaluation of, 95; defeat of Italian army invading Greece, 95; successes in Italian Albania, 95; surrender to Germans, 95

Patch, General Alexander, M., Jr.: author's evaluation of, 12; as commander of U.S. Seventh Army, 12; in operations in Alsace, Rhineland, and southern Germany, 12; in pursuit of Germans up Rhine Valley, 12

Patton, General George S., Jr.: author's evaluation of, 11; in Battle of the Bulge, 10; capture of Palermo, 10; as commander of Western Task Force, 9; crosses Rhine River, 11; in Normandy invasion, 10; in Rhineland, 10; reinstated as commander of American Third Army, 10; relieved of command, 9, 10

Raeder, Grand Admiral Erich: author's evaluation of, 112; builds up German naval strength, 112; as navy chief of staff, 112; as commander in chief of German Army, 112; differences with Hitler, 112; resigns command, 112; convicted of war crimes, 112

Ramsay, Admiral Sir Bertram H.: author's evaluation of, throughout; as commander of naval forces, invasion of Norway, 70; death of, 70; and evacuation of troops from Dunkirk, 69; as Flag Officer, 69;

in invasions of Sicily and Italy, 69; recall to service, 69; retirement, 69

Rommel, Field Marshal Erwin: at Ardennes, 102; author's evaluation of, 105, 106; as commander of Hitler's headquarters, 102; as commander of Afrika Korps, 102; defeated at El Alamein, 103; as group commander in defense of Holland, 105; involvement in plot against Hitler, 105; in northern France, 102; retreat across Libya, 103; suicide of, 105; in Tunisia, 103, 104

Rundstedt, Field Marshal Karl Rudolph von: author's evaluation of, 99; as commander in invasion against West, 97; as commander in invasion of Poland, 97; as commander in invasion of Russia, 97; differences with Hitler, 97; dismissed from command, 97; recalled as commander in chief, West, 99

Russian generals mentioned: Chuikov, Vasili I.; Sokolovski, Vasili D.; Rokossovski, Konstantin K.; Vasilevski, A. M.; Voronov, General N., 86

Simpson, General William H.: author's evaluation of, 11; chosen by Montgomery to spearhead drive into Central Germany, 11

Slessor, Deputy Air Commander in Chief John C.: author's evaluation of, 81

Slim, Field Marshal Sir William Joseph: author's evaluation of, 61; as commander of British Fourteenth Army, 61; in East Africa, 61; return to Burma, 61; in W.W. I, 60; as writer, 61

Smigly-Rydz, Marshal: author's evaluation of, 94; as commander of Polish army, 94

Smith, General Holland M.: controversy with Army Major Ralph C. Smith, 39, 40; in invasion of Saipan; as overall commander of ground assault forces in the Gilberts, Marshalls, Marianas, and at Iwo Jima, 39

Somerville, Admiral of the Fleet Sir James F.: author's evaluation of, throughout; as commander of British fleet in Indian Ocean, 68, 69; as head of British naval delegation in Washington, D.C., 68; with Malay convoys, 68; retirement, 67; sent to Gibraltor, 67; and sinking of the

Bismark, 67; and sinking of French warships, 67

Spaatz, General Carl: author's evaluation of, 47; as Chief of Staff of the U.S. Air Force, 47; as commander of air operations in North Africa, 46; as commander of U.S. Eighth Air Force, 46; as commander of U.S. Strategic Air Force, 46; as director of U.S. strategic bombardment of Japan, 46

Spruance, Admiral Raymond A.: author's evaluation of, throughout; in Battle of Midway, 30; in Battle of the Philippine Sea, 30; as commander of Fifth Fleet, 30; under Kamikaze attack off Okinawa, 30

Stilwell, General Joseph W.: author's evaluation of, 21, 22; and Chiang Kai-shek, 20; as commander of American, China, Burma, India Theaters, 21; defeat in Burma, 20; detractors and enemies of, 21, 22; and Gen. Claire L. Chennault, 22; and responsibility for victory in Burma, 20

Tanaka, Lieutenant General Shinichi: author's evaluation of, 118, 119; and Japanese withdrawal from Thailand, 118, 119

Tassigny, General Jean de Lattre de: in Algiers, 88; author's evaluation of, 88; in Battle of France, 87; as commander of First French Army, 88; as commander of French expeditionary force, 88; with Dever's 6th Army Group, 88; escape to England, 88; imprisonment of, 88; in Riff War, 87; in W.W. I, 87

Tedder, Marshal of the RAF Sir Arthur William: author's evaluation of, 78, 79; as Commander in Chief, Allied Mediterranean Air Command, 79; as Deputy Air Commander in Chief, Allied Mediterranean Air Command, 79; as Deputy Supreme Allied Commander for invasion of Europe, 79; with Royal Flying Corps, W.W. I, 78; technical experience between wars, 78

Timoshenko, Marshal Semën K.: author's evaluation of, 86

Toyoda, Admiral Soemu: author's evaluation of, 116; as Commander of Japanese Combined Air Fleet, 115; defeat in the Philippines, 116; and losses in Battle of

Philippine Sea, 115; and "Sho" (victory) naval plan, 116

Truscott, General Lucian K.: author's evaluation of, 15; as brigade commander in North Africa; as commander of Fifth Army in Italy, 15; as commander of Third Infantry Division in Sicily and Italy, 14; in invasion of southern France, 14, 15; as Sixth Corps commander of Anzio and in Rome campaigns, 14

Turner, Admiral Richard K.: author's evaluation of, 35; as director of amphibious warfare in South and Central Pacific, 35; in Guadalcanal campaign, 35

Umberto, Marshal Pietro: and surrender of East Africa, 120; as viceroy of East Africa, 119

U. S. Navy: role in the Atlantic and Mediterranean, 36

Vandenberg, General Hoyt S.: as Chief of Staff of the Twelfth Air Force, 47; as commander of the Ninth Air Force, 47; as tactical air force commander, 47

Vandergrift, General Alexander A.: author's evaluation of, 40; as commander of First Marine Division on Guadalcanal, 40

Vereker, General Lord John, 6th Viscount Gort: author's evaluation of, 49, 50; as Chief of Imperial General Staff, 49; as commander of British Expeditionary Staff, 49; as commander of Malta, 50; dependence on French methods of warfare, 50; lack of knowledge of modern military developments, 50; and withdrawal to Dunkirk, 50; in World War I, 50

Vian, Sir Philip, and others: author's evaluation of, 72

Voroshilov, Marshal Kliment E.: author's evaluation of, 86

Wainwright, General Jonathan M., IV: author's evaluation of, 19; as commander of all forces in the Philippines, 19; as commander of MacArthur's First Corps in Philippines, 18; in defense of Bataan, 19; with MacArthur at Japanese surrender, 19; and surrender of Bataan and Corregidor, 19

Wavell, Field Marshal Archibald P.: author's evaluation of, throughout; against Vichy-French in Syria, 52; appointed Viceroy of India, 53; in command of troops in Southeast Asia and East Indies, 52; as Commander in Chief of Middle East Command, 50, 51; defeated by Rommel, 52; differences with Churchill, 52; relieved of command, 52; in World War I, 50

Wedemeyer, General Albert C.: author's evaluation of, 27; appointed successor to Stilwell as Chief of Staff to Chiang Kai-shek and commander of American forces in China, 25; as military diplomat, 26; as strategic planner, 25

Weygand, General Maxime: author's evaluation of, 86

Wilson, General Henry M.: author's evaluation of, 53; as British Chiefs of Staff representative in Washington, 53; in command of forces in Persia and Iraq, 53; as commander of Middle East and Mediterranean forces, 53; as commander of Ninth Army, 53; as leader of expeditionary force to Greece, 53; and victory over Italians in Libya, 53; and winning of Syria, 53

Yamamoto, Admiral Isoroku: and attack on Pearl Harbor, 113; author's evaluation of, 114; as Chief of Japan's Combined Fleet, 113; death of, 114; develops Japanese naval air power, 113; in Russo-Japanese War, 113; in W.W. I, 113

Yamashita, General Tomoyuki: author's evaluation of, 117; and conquest of Singapore, 117; and invasion of Malaya, 117; tried as war criminal, 117, 118

Zhukov, Field Marshal Georgi K.: author's evaluation of, 83; as Chief of Staff of Russian army, 84; as commander of Russian forces in Mongolia, 83; as commander in northern regions, 85; as commander of offensive against Berlin, 85; in Russian civil war, 83; at Stalingrad, 85; "Stalin's handyman," 84; in W.W. I, 83